THE
# PICTISH
# TRAIL

## A TRAVELLERS GUIDE
## TO THE OLD PICTISH KINGDOMS

## ANTHONY JACKSON

**THE
ORKNEY
PRESS**

The Orkney Press Ltd.
12 Craigiefield Park,
St Ola, Kirkwall, Orkney.

Published 1989.

ISBN 0 907618 18 9

Editorial Supervision: Howie Firth
Edited by Pam Beasant.
Designed by Iain Ashman

Illustrations by
Iain Ashman and
Helen Jackson

Maps by the
Geography Department
Reprographic Unit,
University of Edinburgh

Cover illustrations show:

Front cover.
L. The Maiden Stone,
 Aberdeenshire: Class II
 No. 17, symbols 23/31*

T.R. Aberlemno 1, Angus
 Class I No. 126,
 symbols 44/5*

B.R. Meigle 6, Perthshire:
 Class II No. 32,
 symbols 3/9

Back cover.
L. Dupplin Cross,
 Perthshire:
 Class III No. 24,
 no symbols

R. Brandsbutt,
 Aberdeenshire:
 Class I No. 108
 symbols 8/45 and oghams

Printed in Orkney
by the Kirkwall Press

The Dunnichen
Stone. (Trail 3)

# Introduction

*"We, the most distant dwellers upon the earth, the last of the*
*free, have been shielded . . . by our remoteness and by the*
*obscurity which has shrouded our name . . . Beyond us lies*
*no nation, nothing but waves and rocks."*

The above quotation, from the northern chieftain Calgacus, encapsulates the isolation and fierce independence of the Picts, who constitute one of the greatest mysteries of Scottish history. Who were they? Where did they come from? Why did they suddenly disappear? We first hear of them from the Roman writers, who describe their fierceness in battle and their later raids on the Roman colony beyond Hadrian's Wall. They survived as an independent people, north of the Forth-Clyde divide, until the days of Kenneth mac Alpin, king of the Scots, who became king of the Picts as well in 843, after which the Picts vanish from history. All that remains is a few fragments: some silver objects, *pit*-placenames (eg Pitlochry), lists of kings — and the symbol stones.

There are hundreds of these stones, scattered all over the east of Scotland, from Fife and Angus to Aberdeen and the north-east, through Moray and Inverness to Ross, Caithness and Sutherland. There are also symbol stones in Orkney and Shetland, as well as in the Western Isles. Despite the distances between all these stones, the strange symbols are remarkably similar, as if they all came from a standardised pattern-book. It seems from the art-style that these symbols came into being at a particular period rather than gradually evolving over the time. But why were they set up? What do the symbols mean? What kind of people were the Picts?

Although comprehensive answers to these questions have not been found, the ideas in this book are put forward as the opening of a door. They have been developed from many years' study of the symbol stones, and they make possible a new insight into the life and society of the Picts. They are a starting point only, however, and it may be that it will be you that takes the next step forward in answering some of the questions that now exist.

By going to see these stones for yourself, you will not only learn more about the Picts, you will journey from busy cities with their collections of stones that do not really belong there, into the farmlands which were once the ancient Pictish kingdoms. You will see parts of Scotland that are off the beaten track — Fowlis Wester and Forteviot, Logierait and Dunfallandy, Menmuir and Aberlemno, Kirktown of Mortlach and Chapel of Garioch. You will also find yourself in out-of-the-way country churchyards, quiet lanes, remote hillside fields and ruined churches. Equally, the quest for the Pictish symbols will take you to some famous buildings such as Falkland Palace, Brechin Cathedral, Dunrobin Castle, Dunkeld Cathedral — and close to others such as the castles of Glamis, Blair, Braemar and Balmoral.

Apart from the locations of the symbol stones and the occasional *pit*-name, we do not know exactly where the Picts lived — although it seems that at one time they inhabited most of northern Scotland. So look out as you go trekking — you may find other Pictish placenames or similar clues.

You make your present rapid way on a journey through the ancient Pictish territory which then took days over the hills and dales. You go from the densely settled and prosperous south where the people clustered near to the rivers and their main means of communication and survival — to the bleaker and more sparsely-populated north where the stones are by the sea. What you will constantly observe is that the stones are never far from water. Why? You will see that the different kingdoms inhabited different territories in their reliance on water: the far north depended on the sea for communication, while the south relied on big rivers. This may explain the distribution of the symbol stones.

The differences between the tamed fields of the southern straths and the unruly countryside of the northern territories may account for the differences between the two major kingdoms of the Picts and their lifestyles. Or the answer may lie in the differing forms of Christianity in these regions, in the differences between the Roman and Celtic churches. Even today, the churches and their graveyards still bear witness to these old foundations.

The trails are each designed to be approximately day-long excursions that minimise the distances between sites, but you can combine them, or just use the details to devise your own itinerary. Remember, however, that if you do decide to do a trail in reverse order, the directions in the British road system are not always the direct opposite of what is given here. Furthermore, although the road directions were correct at the time of writing, alterations do get made, and road numbers can be changed. We cannot always guarantee that the road numbers are the same, but the roads should still be there.

As the original purpose of the stones was lost after the Scots gained power — presumably since it was something that did not apply to them — the stones were soon either abandoned or neglected. They were used as building material, or drain covers, or left to weather. Some stones were rediscovered in the 19th century and moved to private gardens, churches or museums. Others, however, remain in their original place where the local people have always regarded them with respect. The present state of the stones depends on the original material used — hard granite or soft sandstone — and also on when they were first exposed to weathering.

The effects of weathering and early vandalism make some stones difficult to decipher, but you should be careful not to damage the stones any further. Do not attempt to scrape off lichen, or mark the engravings in any way; do not attempt to wash them clean. The surfaces are so fragile that it would take very little to ruin them completely. If you are concerned, write or contact the local museum. The hope is that increased interest in the stones may lead to efforts to preserve these national monuments. An example of one possible way forward comes from Dundee, where a glass-fibre replica has been erected on Dunnichen village green while the real stone is safe in Dundee Museum.

Some of the stones are in agricultural fields, and these are indicated. Here you have a responsibility not to cross standing crops to reach the stone.

You may find that some of the stones are extremely difficult to photograph properly, as they need exactly the correct incidence of slanting light to show up the engravings to their best advantage. If the stone is outside, you may have to come back when the sun is in a better position — you may find that a compass is helpful to calculate when is the best time. It is always advisable to take a flash with you, preferably a detachable one. The problems of photographing the stones are always a challenge, and if you think you have a really good shot, then the

publishers of this book would be interested to see your efforts.

# Who were the Picts?

The name "Pict" was first used by the Romans at the time when they had been ruling southern Britain for more than two centuries. A Roman called Eumenius is the source of the oldest reference we have to the Picti, whom he associates with the Irish as the enemies of the Britons.

As "pictus" is the Latin for "painted", the question has long been asked as to whether Eumenius was describing painted or tattooed people, or whether he was using a Latinised form of a native name. Whatever the reason, in the years after the mention by Eumenius, the Picts reappear in various accounts by other authors. There are descriptions of attacks on the Roman province of Britain by Picts, Scots and Saxons, and accounts of measures taken by the Romans to strengthen their defences against the threat from the north.

The Romans had first landed in Britain in 55 BC under Julius Caesar, but only made their annexation in the following century, when the emperor Claudius landed with an army in 43 AD. From the bridgehead in southern Britain, Roman power spread steadily outwards, reaching the line of Tyne and Solway by the end of 78 AD. Under the governorship of the Roman general Julius Agricola, the legions moved into what is present-day Scotland, occupying first the lowlands and then pushing north through Perthshire and the Tay valley. In 84 AD, Agricola won a resounding victory over the native "Caledonians", as they were called by the Romans, at a site which is still unidentified but which may be as far north as Forres.

The Romans were either unwilling or unable to hold the line so far north, and retrenched to the Tyne-Solway frontier where Hadrian's Wall was commenced around 120 AD. The frontier was then pushed north again by Hadrian's heir, Antoninus, whose own wall between the Forth and the Clyde was begun around 143 AD.

Although the peoples north of the Antonine Wall were never brought under Roman rule, there were long periods of peace between the various incursions that brought the area to the attention of chroniclers. But from about 360 AD onwards, as the pressures on the Roman Empire increased, the Picts became more prominent in descriptions of raids and border conflict. Attacks on Roman Britain in 368 were recorded by the Roman writer Ammianus Marcellinus thus: "It will be enough to say that at that time Picts, divided into two tribes . . . were creating great havoc."

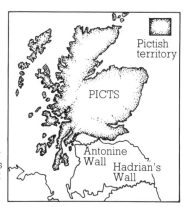

Pictish territory

PICTS

Extent of territory occupied by Picts when Romans left Britain in AD 410

Antonine Wall

Hadrian's Wall

## The territory of the Picts

From the Roman accounts of their problems with the Picts, it seems that Pictish territory was essentially north of the Forth-Clyde line, beyond the Antonine Wall. How widely spread the Picts were within that area is less clear. The eastern side of Scotland is where we find the majority of the clues to Pictish settlement, in the form of symbol stones and *pit*-placenames. Several hundred of these names, such as Pitlochry, Pittenweem and Pitmeddan, are found to the east and north-east, usually not too far from a riverside or sea coast, although the *pit*-names do not seem to extend to the symbol stone territory of the Northern and Western Isles.

Any Pictish presence in the Argyll area would have waned rapidly after about 500 AD, when people from a small Irish kingdom on the coast of Antrim crossed the short stretch of sea that separated them from the peninsula of Kintyre. They seem to have come as allies of the British of the lands around the Clyde, who may have been glad to have someone to shield them from one area of attack. The new people were the Scotti of Dal Riada, whose power was consolidated in the later part of the 6th century under the guidance of the Irish missionary, Columba.

After the high point of the Columban period, Scottish fortunes gradually declined, with defeats sustained at the hands of several of the other peoples of the time. But Dal Riada survived, and by the late 8th century there seem to have been examples of intermarriage between ruling familes of Picts and Scots. Around 800 it was also recorded by Nennius that "the Irish (i.e. the Scots), who are in the West, and the Picts from the north, fought together in a united assault on the British unremittingly". It is possible that one or two rulers of the one group may have also held power over the other, but the final permanent union was sealed in 843 under a Scottish king, Kenneth mac Alpin (son of Alpin).

The union came at a time when both Picts and Scots were under pressure from the sea-borne attacks of the Vikings, at whose hands the Picts had already suffered a crushing defeat. Kenneth's achievement was to weld the two peoples into a unit which was strong enough to survive the pressures on its various frontiers, and grow into the future country of Scotland. To do so he had to take stern measures to exert power over the Picts. This may be the grim background to the setting up of the monument known as Sueno's Stone which depicts scenes of slaughter of men in multiples of seven, a figure of particular significance to the organisation of the Pictish kingdom.

However Kenneth enforced his rule, this is the time during which the Picts as a separate people began to fade away from history, leaving behind only a few clues as to their life and society — among them the symbol stones.

## Sueno's Stone

Sueno's Stone (which means "Sven's Stone") is the largest Pictish sculptured stone, and lies just outside Forres, not far from the old fortress at Burghead, in the county of Moray — the central area of the northern Pictish territory. The stone is 20 feet high, with an enormous cross on one side and nearly a hundred figures on the other. It is a Class III stone on which the carving and design are definitely Pictish, and it dates from around the 9th century.

The stone depicts scenes of fighting and killing, including the bodies of decapitated prisoners. From the scale of the stone, it must have been erected to mark a major event, such as the alleged slaughter of the Pictish nobles in a single treacherous attack by Kenneth mac Alpin. The stone shows dead bodies lying in two groups of seven which would then be the leaders of the northern and the southern Picts. Sited on the border of the old Pictish kingdom of Moray, the stone would be a grim reminder of the strength of the new unified state forged by Kenneth.

## The Pictish king-lists

One useful source of information about the Picts comes from the monastic chroniclers. They had tables to set out for them the particular date on which Easter had been calculated to fall, and they often used the space in the margin of each year's entry to record particular events of significance for that year. Among such events were the succession or deaths of kings. Together with various other lists, these documents give us details of some of the Pictish rulers, although to reconcile the sometimes differing references in different lists is a difficult task.

When we compare Pictish king-lists with those for the Scots of Dal Riada, we find an immediate and major contrast. Among the Scots, one brother may succeed another one, and a son may succeed his father. But among the Picts, although one brother may follow another, no son succeeds his father until the very end of the Pictish line. The Northumbrian historian, Bede, whose own monastery of Jarrow was in close touch with the Picts, says that the Pictish succession went not through the male line but the female one, and the evidence of the king-lists confirms this. He also speaks of "northern Picts" and "southern Picts", which suggests that by his time (he finished his history in 731 AD) the Picts were divided into two sub-kingdoms.

Some of the Pictish kings are known from descriptions in chronicles of the time. We learn from Columba's biographer, Adomnan, of the journey of the saint to the court in Inverness of the Pictish king, Bridei, son of Maelchon. Bede calls Bridei "an exceptionally powerful king", and it is clear that he stemmed for a time the encroachment of the Scots of Dal

Riada. Bridei, who ruled from about 554 to 584, was the son of a powerful father, for "Maelchon" was in fact the great king Maelgwyn, who ruled in Gwynedd, in north-west Wales. The fact that a number of fathers of Pictish kings came from further afield is further evidence for Bede's emphasis of the importance of succession through the Pictish female line.

Inheritance through the female, rather than the male, line is not unique to the Picts. There are examples of it in various societies in different parts of the world today, although it is of course not nearly as common as the system of male descent that we are used to in most of the Western world. Inheritance through the female line has a number of consequences for the pattern of life in a society, and this is something that we will study carefully in this book.

## The king-list manuscripts

We often have to get our information about the Pictish kings at second hand. Most of the early Easter tables were destroyed or lost, so the annal notes that were made on them have only come down to us as copies from the original, or copies of the copies.

The manuscripts which we have today are sometimes surprisingly recent. For example, of the two great Irish annal collections, the principal manuscript of the Annals of Tigernach was written down in the 14th century, and that of the Annals of Ulster in the 15th century.

Another valuable source is a collection of texts compiled and written in York in the 14th century, under the direction of Robert of Poppleton, who is believed to have been a Carmelite friar. The manuscript, now in the National Library of Paris, sets out a list of Pictish kings. The following is the entry about Bridei, son of Maelchon:

*"Bridei filius Mailcon xxx annis regnauit. In octauo anno regni eius baptizatus est a sancto Colmba."*
*"Bridei, son of Maelchon, reigned for 30 years. In the 8th year of his reign he was baptised by Saint Columba."*

Other entries are even shorter:

*"Bridei filius Bili xxi annis regnauit."*
*"Bridei, son of Bili, reigned for 21 years."*

*"Taran filius Entifidich iiii annis regnauit."*
*"Tarain, son of Ainftech, reigned for 4 years."*

This latter Bridei was also one of the great Pictish kings, whom we shall meet later. In the meantime, note that his successor, Tarain, was not his son.

# The symbols on the stones

There are three main types of Pictish stone monuments. Class I stones are the simplest, with only symbols on them, cut into their surface. Class II stones also have symbols, but Celtic ornamentation as well, and their designs are in relief. On Class III stones there are figures of men and beasts in relief, but no symbols of the kind found on Classes I and II.

What we will be studying here will be mainly the stones of Classes I and II and their symbols. We start with Class I, where we have the symbols on their own, without extraneous designs. And here one of the first and most important things to note is that on almost every single undamaged stone the symbols come in pairs, almost touching each other. The one symbol that does not follow this rule is the so-called mirror-and-comb, but this turns out to follow a well-defined rule of its own. It is always placed at the bottom of a pair of symbols, almost touching the lower one. We shall see shortly how its rôle can be interpreted in the pairing of the other symbols.

There are a number of designs that only occur once on Class I stones, and there are a number that occur only on the stones of Class II. But apart from these, all the other designs fall into a core of only 28 symbols, together with the mirror-and-comb.

## *Three classes of symbol stone*

On Class I stones, the symbols are cut into the stone. Class I stones are often rough boulders, or crudely-shaped local stones of sandstone or granite.

▼

Class I:
Strathpeffer

Class II:
Meigle 6

Class III:
Edderton

▲
The work on Class II stones is more elaborate; the stones have been dressed so that the symbols stand out in relief. Additional figures are present as well, and there is a cross on the other side.

Class III stones have no ▶ symbols. They have other figures and a cross.

### Class III stones

Class III stones are the last Pictish carved stones to be erected. They date from the period c.790-840. They are similar to Class II in that they are dressed stones with a Christian cross and many other carved figures, but there are now no Pictish symbols.

The significance of these stones is that they witness the triumph of Christian-approved marriages and the demise of the old Pictish lineage alliances. In other words, there has been a shift towards patrilinear succession (in which descent is traced from father to son) — the norm for Scots who, by this time, were largely in control of the Pictish territory.

On Class III stones, as on Class II, there are often horsemen. The majority of the horsemen are in Angus and Perth, in the southern kingdom of the Picts. This was the power-base of Bridei, son of Bili, after he defeated the Northumbrians at Nechtansmere (see "The origin of the symbol stones" section). The horsemen seem to be a symbol of royal power. On Class II stones, they are usually hunting horsemen, but as we progress to Class III we get a mix of hunters and armed warriors. We seem to be moving from a peaceful period when the Pictish royal alliances were still intact, into a more divided time. It may be significant that nearly all the armed horsemen in Class III in Angus, Perth and Fife are crudely carved, perhaps representing an alien tradition. Just as the older symbol stones had carried a message from the Pictish king or overlord, so too could later stones carved under the Scottish influence.

## The classification of the symbols

Public attention was first brought to the overall quantity and quality of the Pictish stones and their symbols by J. Stuart's two volumes of *The Sculptured Stones of Scotland* (1856 and 1867). It was magnificently illustrated with sketches, reproduced in sepia wash, of some 300 stones (not all of them Pictish), and it contains more than half the stones we know about today. The book awoke such interest in Pictish stones that four or five new ones were reported each year up to the turn of the century.

Attempts to systematise the stones resulted in a book which is an all-time classic of Pictish studies: *The Early Christian Monuments of Scotland,* by Romilly Allen and Joseph Anderson. It was Anderson who first suggested that the Pictish stones could be grouped into three classes, while Allen set out the animal and geometrical designs of Classes I and II in a numbered list. Thus the crescent-and-V-rod is described by the number 8, while the double-disc-and-Z-rod is 5. The salmon is 41 and the serpent 44.

The basic core of 28 symbols are all in Allen's list, except in three cases it turns out on closer examination that one of the items on his list may in fact be two similar, but separate, symbols; and in two cases he may have taken two forms of a particular symbol to be separate. So, for instance, his 40 becomes a goose (40g) and an eagle (40e), while his sea-horses, 42 and 43, seem to be the same, 42/43.

## The basic set of symbols

The basic set of 28 symbols can be set out in some particularly structured ways, by applying simple methods of ordering. Some symbols are much more frequent than others, and it is possible to bring this out in a diagram, while also bringing out the classification of symbols into geometrical and animal, with the geometrical being further subdivided into rodded and unrodded.

Setting out the symbols with the most frequent ones being in the top right of the diagram, we find that they form a pattern of four sets of seven. The most frequent symbol on the stones is the crescent-and-V-rod (8), found in 75% of all pairs. Next comes the double-disc-and-Z-rod (5), which occurs in 40% of the pairings. Both these symbols are in the top right-hand set A in the diagram, and the extent of the significance of the seven symbols of A is illustrated by the fact that no less than 80% of all the pairings consist purely of two of these seven symbols.

The diagram shows how the rodded symbols — in A — contrast with their unrodded counterparts in B. There is also the balance between the alternating lines of geometrical and animal symbols, with the basic 28 symbols comprising 16 geometrical and 12 animal.

Taken together, the 14 symbols of sets A and B account for no less than 98% of all pairings.

It is thus clear that the paired symbols form a system with a great deal of structure. But why should anyone want to set up such a system? And why should it be displayed on stones in Pictish Scotland and nowhere else? To find the answer, we shall look now at an aspect of human life in society where pairings are important and where such pairings are regulated in some circumstances to form a structure which can be complex.

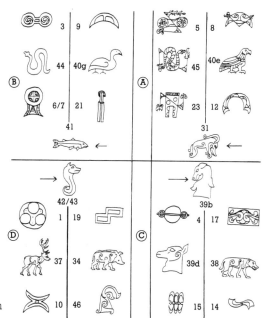

The basic 28 symbols arranged in 4 sets of 7.

# The Pictish symbol designs
(according to Romilly Allen and Joseph Anderson)

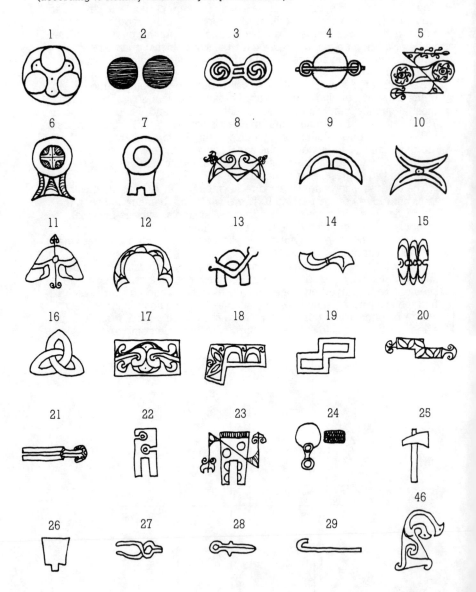

Geometric designs

Animal designs

### The Burghead Bulls

In Moray, near the old Pictish fort of Burghead, several small Pictish stone tablets were discovered incised with a single design of a bull. This design was originally numbered 32 in the 1903 listing, but closer examination shows that there are two forms: a bull (32b) and a cow (32c). The cows are found near other Pictish forts in Inverness and the East Lomond hills, while the bulls are all in Burghead. These designs always occur singly. They are unique in this characteristic of never combining with another symbol. What is the significance of this?

The answer may lie in the discovery of some 30 examples of these smallish stones with engraved bulls, found during the period of the rebuilding of Burghead harbour, next to the site of the old Pictish fort. There is no other instance of so many Pictish designs being found in a single place, and this suggests that they were deliberately thrown into the sea. It was a common practice among Iron Age people (including the Celts) to put offerings into water (wells, lakes and rivers) to the guardian deity, in the hope of receiving a blessing. It seems possible that this was the purpose of the Burghead bulls — a dedication for the fertility of local herds of cattle. A tradition of bull-sacrifice in this area into the 18th century is recorded.

# Tracing descent

We live in families, through which things are passed on from one generation to the next. Some things, like the family surname, tend to go through the male side of the family. For instance, in most Western countries, a woman on marriage traditionally gives up her own original surname, and takes up instead the surname of her husband. The children of the marriage take up this surname as well when they arrive.

Another way of looking at marriages and surnames is to say that our society consists of lineages, each with its own symbol or name, and when a woman marries she can be thought of as transferring from one lineage to another. The children of the marriage belong to the lineage of the father. This is a system where descent is reckoned through the male line, a system of patrilinear descent. We can show what happens through a diagram.

A man from one lineage (shaded dark) marries a woman from another (unshaded).

The children of the marriage belong to the father's lineage.

When the time comes for the daughter to get married, she leaves the lineage.

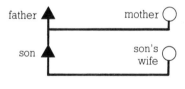

And when the son gets married, the lineage is joined by his wife.

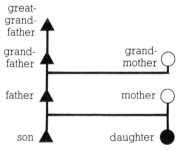

So, as the years go by, the lineage is seen to consist of the male line, together with the women they bring in from other lineages on marriage, and the children produced by the marriages.

Now it is perfectly possible to imagine the opposite type of system, in which the surname is determined by the mother, rather than the father. We can illustrate this by going through the sequence of diagrams again, transferring on marriage the men, rather than the women.

male / female

A man from one lineage marries a woman from another.

father / mother
son / daughter

The children of the marriage belong to the mother's lineage.

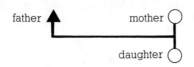

father / mother
daughter

When the time comes for the son to get married, he leaves the lineage. The daughter remains.

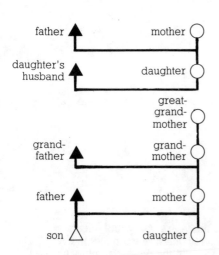

father / mother
daughter's husband / daughter

And when the daughter gets married her husband joins the lineage.

great-grand-mother
grand-father / grand-mother
father / mother
son / daughter

So, as the years go by, the continuity of the lineage is through the female side. The women form the core of the lineage, which consists of them, the men they marry, and the children they produce.

This kind of system, in which descent is reckoned through the female side, is called matrilinear. An extreme case of it would be if women held power as well, which would be handed down by the descent system from each woman to her daughter. This kind of society, called a matriarchy, would be a mirror-image of our traditionally male-dominated society, and there are arguments as to whether or not such a society has ever existed. In the various matrilinear societies that have been observed, the men still retain power.

The difference between them and us is that power is not passed on by a man to his son, but goes instead through the female line, to his sister's son.

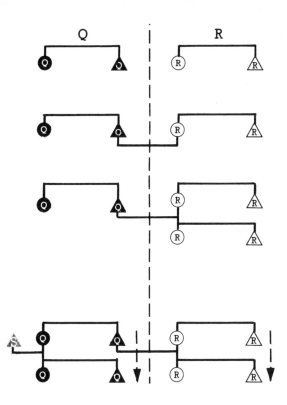

We start with the chief of lineage Q and his sister; likewise for lineage R.

The chief of lineage Q marries a wife from lineage R.

The children of this marriage belong to lineage R. So they cannot inherit the chieftainship of lineage Q from their father. The chieftainship has to remain within the lineage.

The next chief of lineage Q will be someone who inherits it by virtue of who his mother was. In other words, it must be the son of a Q-woman of the appropriate family. Thus, after a chief dies, his power passes to his sister's sons.

There are a number of examples of matrilinear descent system that still survive in the modern world, and they are of interest in their own right. But the crucial importance of the matrilinear system for us is that it was the system of inheritance used by the Picts.

# Marriage systems

You can see that a marriage results in a gain and a loss, depending on which lineage gets the children. The question still asked today is: are we gaining a daughter or losing a son? But the longer-term gain goes to the lineage that gets the children of the union.

To keep the balance, the accounts must be squared. One way of doing this is to make a payment of some form at the time of the marriage. Another is to make the repayment in kind, in the form of a marriage in the other direction in the next generation.

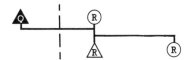

A man from Q marries a woman from R. The gain for lineage R out of this marriage is two children.

In the next generation, the debt is repaid, when the male R-child marries back into the Qs. He marries his cross-cousin on his mother's side.

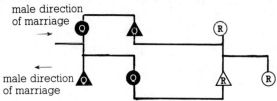

male direction of marriage
→

←
male direction of marriage

Clearly, this pattern can continue through the generations, with the direction of marriage alternating with each generation.

**Males**

1st generation  Q → R
2nd generation  Q ← R
3rd generation  Q → R

So far, we have only married off half of each generation. What do we do with the other half?

One possibility is to let them marry each other in the same way. In other words, a very tight system of links between Q and R would develop, with every member of the one lineage being restricted to marrying the appropriate cross-cousin.

**Males**

1st generation  Q ⇌ R
2nd generation  Q ⇄ R
3rd generation  Q ⇌ R

Another possibility would be to bring in a third lineage.

**Males**

1st generation  P → Q → R → P
2nd generation  P ← Q ← R ← P
3rd generation  P → Q → R → P

But the pattern most often found is to intermarry in groups of four lineages.

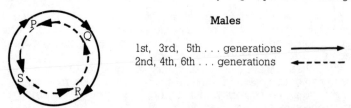

**Males**

1st, 3rd, 5th . . . generations  ⟶
2nd, 4th, 6th . . . generations  ⟵ - - - -

It may be that to intermarry between just two lineages gives too small a pool, and that to intermarry in threes is not quite so symmetrical in appearance. Whatever the reason for the pattern, the grouping of lineages in fours for this kind of marriage is what is most often found in practice, and sometimes appears in creation myths where peoples speak of their emergence from four founding ancestors.

# Lineages and symbols

When lineages group together in systems of marriage exchange, we can sum up what happens by a little shorthand notation, describing the marriage of Q-women and R-men by writing it down as Q/R.

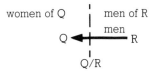

If there were no restrictions on marriage between one lineage and another, there would be twelve possible marriages in each generation. We can see this more clearly by looking at the various combinations of the symbols P, Q, R and S.

|   | P   | Q   | R   | S   |
|---|-----|-----|-----|-----|
| P | P/P |     |     |     |
| Q |     | Q/Q |     |     |
| R |     |     | R/R |     |
| S |     |     |     | S/S |

Allowed P/Q, P/R P/S,
Q/P Q/R Q/S
R/P R/Q R/S
S/P S/Q S/R

Forbidden P/P Q/Q R/R S/S

Marriage within a lineage, i.e. between brother and sister, is not allowed. Hence four of the possible 16 combinations of the symbols do not appear.

In the kind of matrilinear society that we have been considering, only marriages of the kind shown by the arrows can take place.

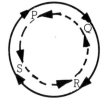

In any particular generation, there are four possible marriages. Alternating with this are another four.

1st, 3rd, 5th generations: S/P P/Q Q/R R/S
2nd, 4th, 6th generations: P/S Q/P R/Q S/R

So, of the 16 possible combinations of the symbols P, Q, R and S, only 8 appear in practice.

Forbidden: P/P Q/Q R/R S/S
P/R R/P Q/S S/Q

To summarise so far: in a matrilinear society, marriage patterns are often complex, and different lineages are often linked together in fours in a system of cross-cousin marriage.

   And this takes us to the key question: given that the Picts were matrilinear, and given that the symbols on the stones come in pairs, are the symbols the marks of lineages, and do the combinations of the symbols represent marriages?

As we look at particular areas, we do seem to see the favouring of some combinations of symbols and the absence of others. For example, on trail number 7 you will come across a number of stones at Rhynie, an important settlement in Pictish times. Among the Rhynie stones are:

Rhynie 1 (96) 41/31    We can show these
Rhynie 4 (93) 31/8+    combinations in a
Rhynie 6 (95) 5/8+     diagram

Of these four symbols — 8, 31, 5 and 41 — other examples are found in the area. Some combinations are found but not others. There are no combinations of 8 and 41, for instance. And no combinations of 5 and 31.

We do find a combination of 8 and 31 (at Kintore, 112). And there was a combination of 8 and 5 at Tillytarmont (79, now moved). The stone in private grounds at Keith Hall (109) combines 5 and 41. So we have:

| 8/5 | 5/41* | 41/31 | 31/8+ |
|---|---|---|---|
| Tillytarmont 2 (79) | Keith Hall (109) | Rhynie 1 (96) | Rhynie 4 (93) |

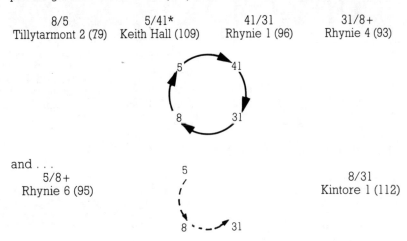

and . . .
5/8+                                8/31
Rhynie 6 (95)                    Kintore 1 (112)

What is beginning to appear is a pattern made up of the four symbols 8, 31, 41 and 5 — a pattern in which some combinations appear and others do not. If this pattern is true, there should be two further stones in the area, both with the symbol 41, one being 41/5, the other 31/41.

And, remarkably, we do find two stones of the required characteristics. The first is Tillytarmont 6 (82b), with the symbols 41/5. While at Barflat, a mile away from Rhynie square, we have a tantalising stone (97), with one symbol broken off. The first symbol is 31 — and there we stop. If we knew what the second symbol had been, we could tell whether or not the pattern was indeed what all the other combinations in the area suggest it is.

But these kinds of patterns do appear again and again in the distribution of symbol stones. The patterns are often incomplete — as we would expect, when over the centuries stones have been lost, removed or broken. But it is remarkable that when there are so many possible combinations of the symbols that could occur in a random distribution, the actual distribution shows concentrations of certain combinations and absence of others.

And since stones are still from time to time being rediscovered, we have a test of the patterns which seems to appear. If a stone turns up in a particular area to complete the pattern, it would be a dramatic confirmation of these ideas. If one turned up with the exact opposite, it would still be interesting, since the new information would help us move to a better interpretation of the existing data.

Thus the importance of any new discovery is crucial. At any time a chance excavation or examination of old records could produce a stone or symbol combination that would tell us we had a definite solution to the mystery of the Picts — and it could be you who finds it!

## *The symbol pairs*

(Class II in brackets)

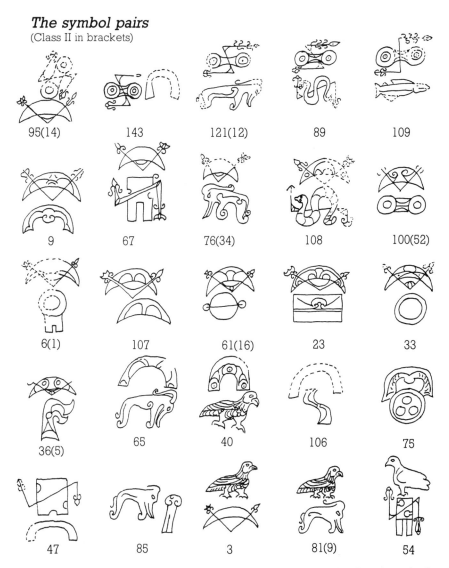

| 95(14) | 143 | 121(12) | 89 | 109 |
| 9 | 67 | 76(34) | 108 | 100(52) |
| 6(1) | 107 | 61(16) | 23 | 33 |
| 36(5) | 65 | 40 | 106 | 75 |
| 47 | 85 | 3 | 81(9) | 54 |

Continued overleaf

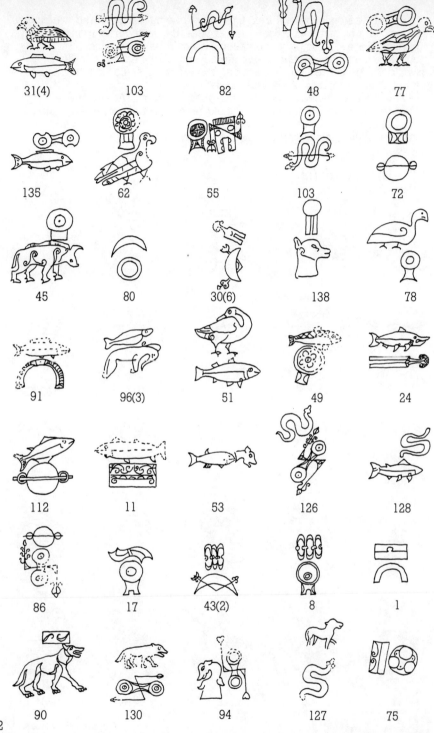

31(4)  103  82  48  77

135  62  55  103  72

45  80  30(6)  138  78

91  96(3)  51  49  24

112  11  53  126  128

86  17  43(2)  8  1

90  130  94  127  75

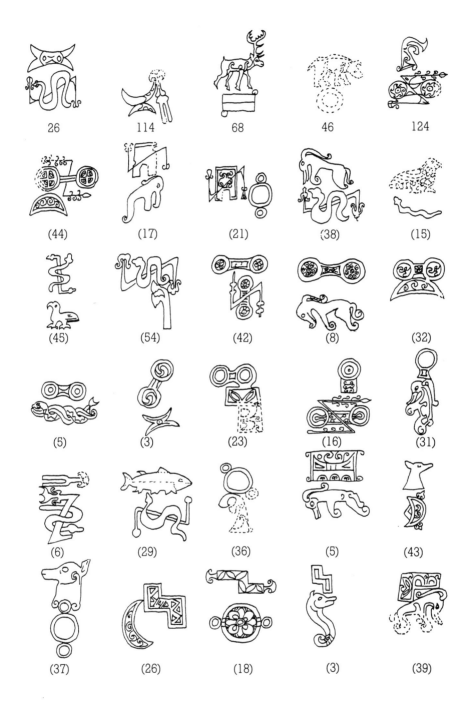

26     114     68     46     124

(44)     (17)     (21)     (38)     (15)

(45)     (54)     (42)     (8)     (32)

(5)     (3)     (23)     (16)     (31)

(6)     (29)     (36)     (5)     (43)

(37)     (26)     (18)     (3)     (39)

## Chiefs and symbols

If lineages group together in fours for intermarrying, there is a very even balance between them all. How can this be made compatible with the idea of hereditary chieftainships?

Suppose, for instance, that lineage Q is to be a dominant lineage.

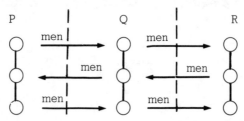

In the 1st generation shown, the Q-chief marries an R-woman. The children are in her lineage, R. In the next generation, one of these male R-children will marry back into the Q-lineage to produce the next Q-generation.

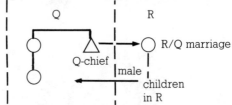

As we go from generation to generation, the Q-chiefs will have first R-fathers, then P-fathers. That is, they will come from Q/R marriages and Q/P marriages alternatingly.

But how can these Q-chiefs retain their status when their fathers belong to lesser lineages?

The answer is to endow the marriage with a payment. When the Q-chief marries into the R-lineage, a payment is made to the R-lineage. The male child of the marriage, although brought up in the lesser R-lineage, is still the son of a Q-chief, and will indeed go on to father a future Q-chief. An endowment to provide for him conveys his status.

We extend our system of marriage notation to cover this situation.

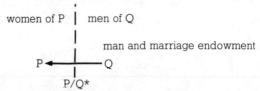

So, of the four possible marriage-combinations of the lineages P, Q and R, we have two involving the payment of a marriage endowment, R/Q* and P/Q*, covering the situation where a Q-chief marries into one of the lesser lineages R and P.

When a man from R or P marries into Q, there is no problem, since the children belong to their mother's lineage Q, and thus inherit appropriate status from her chieftainly lineage.

We can now further note that the lineage Q does not intermarry directly with the fourth lineage in the group, S.

That might seem at first sight to reduce the status of S on the grounds that it is more distant from the chieftainly lineage Q than even the lesser lineages R and P. But we could turn that argument round by saying that a mark of being a Q-member is that you cannot marry anyone else from Q. In other words, there can be an implication that S-members are excluded from marrying Q-members precisely because they are in some way akin. So it is consistent to have a structure to this group in which the lineage S forms a kind of level of sub-chiefs.

So we end up with this pattern of marriages:

1st, 3rd, 5th generations . . . S/P  P/Q*  Q/R  R/S+
2nd, 4th, 6th generations . . . P/S+  Q/P  R/Q*  S/R

where the R/S+ notation denotes a marriage endowment from lineage S to lineage R on the occasion of the marriage of a subchief from S to a woman from the lesser lineage R.
    As the S lineage is not so high in status as the chieftainly lineage Q, the payment on the marriage of an S-chief into R or P is not so much as when a Q-chief marries into them.

If we now go back to the Pictish symbols on the stones, we have a possible explanation for the mirror-and-comb and the mirror on its own. They mark marriages where a lineage of chiefs or sub-chiefs marries a lesser lineage and must pay bridewealth.
    If we now go back to the stones we studied in the Rhynie area, we can see how such a system would work.

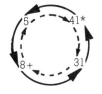

* Chieftainly lineage
(with mirror-and-comb)

+ Lineage of sub-chiefs
(with mirror only)

| 8/5 | 5/41* | 41/31 | 31/8+ |
|---|---|---|---|
| Tillytarmont 2 (79) | Keith Hall (109) | Rhynie 1 (96) | Rhynie 4 (93) |
| 5/8+ | 41/5 | 31/? | 8/31 |
| Rhynie 6 (95) | Tillytarmont 6 (82b) | Barflat (97) | Kintore 1 (112) |

We saw before that it was quite remarkable that we could find certain combinations of the four symbols present while other combinations were missing. What is even more remarkable is that the mirror-and-comb and mirror symbols can be fitted into this system as well. The tantalising broken stone at Barflat becomes even more tantalising — the prediction of this theory is that the missing symbols are 41*. A 31/41* combination at Barflat would complete this pattern exactly.

# The origin of the symbol stones

Thus far, then, we have seen that the combinations of the Pictish symbols reproduce exactly in symbolic form the marriage-patterns of a society where inheritance is through the mother's side — a distinguishing characteristic of the Picts noted by various of their contemporaries. But why should they want to inscribe these marriage-patterns in stone, and set them up for all to see?

Art historians, looking closely at the workmanship, suggest that from the similarity of the inscribed symbols they were all cut at about the same time, somewhere about the 7th century. It looks as if an overall decision was made that the symbols should be incised on stones all over the Pictish territory, an action consistent with a decree of a strong king.

In the 7th century, the Picts were ruled for a time by one of their greatest kings, a man who was one of the most powerful figures of the period, and who won one of the most decisive battles in the history of the country which is now called Scotland.

His name was Bridei, whose father, Bili, was king of the Britons of Strathclyde, whose capital was Dumbarton. The matrilineal system of the Picts would have brought Bridei to power through his mother's position as, presumably, a member of the Pictish royal house. Royal blood on his father's side would no doubt have been an asset to his claims to overlordship of the Picts; it may have come about as part of a marriage-alliance.

The Picts needed a strong ruler at the time of Bridei's succession in 671, as they faced a formidable threat from Northumbria. The Angles of Northumbria had gradually increased their power over the previous century, reaching northwards into the Lothian area which they took over after besieging Edinburgh in 638. The Picts, on the north side of the Forth, felt Northumbrian influence to the extent of acknowledging Northumbrian overlordship.

Under Bridei, however, the Picts asserted their independence, and maintained it against the threat from the south. There are accounts of various military adventures in the early 680s which suggest that Bridei was consolidating his power in various parts of his territory, including the Orkney Islands in the north which he is recorded as laying waste in 682.

In the year 685, the Northumbrian king, Ecgfrith, led an army north to subdue the Picts, and Bridei faced one of the most efficient fighting forces of the time. He avoided confrontation for a while, allowing the Northumbrians to cross first the Forth, and then the Earn and Tay, to come up Strathmore to difficult, swampy ground near the fortress of Dunnichen. Ecgfrith and a large part of his army fell at the battle of Dunnichen Moss or Nechtansmere, and Northumbrian domination of the north was averted.

It is clear that in order to prepare for this encounter, Bridei would have had to enforce his authority over the whole of the Pictish territory. In the years between his succession and Nechtansmere, any division among the Picts would have been an opportunity for exploitation by Ecgfrith. To settle any arguments about marriage-patterns among Pictish lineages, and to record formally the alliances and chieftainships that were involved, would have been a logical way of strengthening the chain of control that ran down through the subkingdoms of his territory. And this may have been the origin of the Class I symbol stones of present-day Scotland.

# The origin of the symbols

We are familiar with the system of lineages among the Scottish clans, where the succession passed from father to son in a patrilinear system. The word "clan" is Irish for "children"; in other words, the clan Donald were the children of Donald, the group of lineages claiming common descent from the ancestor Donald. Today we associate clans with a particular design of tartan, which may be a recent invention, but there were older distinguishing symbols, such as particular plants.

In other parts of the world, lineages also distinguish themselves by particular totemic symbols, often derived from animals or plants. The choice of such symbols depends not so much on the intrinsic properties of the animal or plant involved, but rather in the particular way in which it differs from another. For example, if one lineage chooses a goose as their emblem and another lineage chooses an eagle, they are really saying that the two lineages are basically similar (both totems are birds) but they differ inasmuch as the eagle is a carnivorous predator that soars in the sky while the goose is a vegetarian living on water. These contrasts in bird behaviour reflect differences between the lineages. For instance, the eagle lineage may be hunters while the goose lineage are agriculturalists. Whether or not the Picts used these particular features to differentiate pairs of lineages is something that we do not know, but this method of similarities and differences is the standard way in which totems are devised, all over the world, so we will follow it here and look at some possible interpretations.

In the division of the symbols into four groups of seven, (see "The basic set of symbols" section), there are a number of contrasting pairs that can be seen, such as the goose and the eagle we have just mentioned. For instance, there is the contrast between rodded and unrodded symbols. What do the rods mean? The contrast between the crescent and the double-disc may be that between the sun and the moon. The bird/serpent motif is well-known from legend and folklore.

The third row of symbols may at first look less receptive to interpretation, but a possible clue comes from the shape of symbols 6/7. It looks very like the Pictish house excavated by Anna Ritchie at Buckquoy in Birsay, Orkney — a circular room with two rectangular leg-like structures. If that was the case, then symbol 21 could be forked lightning, especially dangerous to thatched roofed houses. The torc-like symbol 12 looks like a rainbow, which heralds the end of rain from heaven, just as lightning heralds the beginning.

But what were the roles of the lineages? The key must be in the V- and Z-rods, as symbols of power. If the V-rod was a divining rod, used for discovering water and other hidden things, then lineage 8 might be skilled foretellers of the future and of such aspects as the rising and setting of the moon. The ability to control tides, and weather and sea conditions, would be a natural thing to attribute to such a lineage, and it is interesting in this context to recall an account of one incident in the life of St Columba. On a visit to the capital of the Pictish king of Inverness, he encountered a court magician who is said to have raised a storm and an enveloping mist to hinder the missionary's voyage on Loch Ness.

The Z-rods may also be associated with power. The broken rod may represent the dead — in other words, the ancestors of the lineage, who could be called on for help and protection in times of need. So, for instance, the Z-rod in symbol 23 may represent the power to protect houses, against, for instance, the threat of lightning.

It is possible that the symbols in sets C and D concern craftsmen. For instance, in the contrasting pairing 17 and 19, symbol 17 looks like a shield and could be a weaponsmith's symbol, while symbol 19, a stepped rectangle, could be a forge. Similarly, 4, a large pot, might represent the potter's skill, while 1, a disc, could be three pots in a circular oven. In other words, the symbols 4 and 17 in set C might represent manufacturing craft skills, while their counterparts in set D might have skills in firing the corresponding furnaces.

There are numerous patterns of similarities and differences in the symbols, and as you encounter the different examples along the road, you will perhaps form your own interpretation of the skills or attributes they may represent.

# The distribution of the symbol stones

When the Class I symbols are gathered together in fours, area by area, it turns out that a total of 32 groups of four cover the whole distribution. The gaps in the groups are a test for the theory, where a newly-uncovered stone may — or may not — fit the prediction. The 32 groups consist of four groups of 8, each spread over the territory of one of the old Pictish kingdoms described in early accounts. The kingdom of Cat covers Shetland, Orkney, the Western Isles, Caithness and Sutherland. Fidach covers the counties of Ross, Inverness, Moray and Banff. Ce is much of the county of Aberdeen; while Circind is the rest of Aberdeen along with Angus. Consistent with this division of the Pictish territory into four parts is the fact that the distribution of the known Class I stones is almost exactly equally divided between the four areas.

When we come to Class II stones, we find that the major presence is in Circind. In fact, there is an even distribution of symbol-groupings between, on the one hand, Circind, and on the other, the three areas of Cat, Fidach and Ce together. The inference is that by Class II times, the distribution of people and power had moved towards the south of the Pictish territory, which had evolved into a unit of two kingdoms; Cat, Fidach and Ce in the north, and Circind in the south. It may be that the erection of the Class II stones was to put on record a modified system of marriage-patterns that had developed in the years after Bridei. But who ordered the work to be done, and why, are questions that you might like to explore as you travel round the ancient Pictish kingdoms and study the history of the period.

Later, we find references to another division of the southern kingdom itself into four sub-units. The northern part was known as Circind (Angus and the Mearns) and Fotla (Atholl and Gowrie); while the south became Fortriu (Strathearn and Menteith) and Fib (Fife and Kinross). We thus have seven names of provinces into which the Pictish territory was divided at one stage, and this may be the time of the origin of the legend that the Picts derived from a king who had seven sons with the names of these regions.

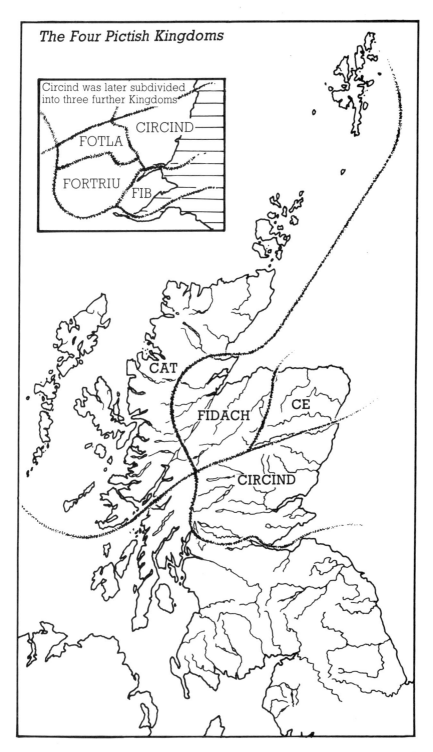

## The Four Pictish Kingdoms

Circind was later subdivided into three further Kingdoms

CIRCIND

FOTLA

FORTRIU

FIB

CAT

FIDACH

CE

CIRCIND

29

# THE PICTISH TRAILS

This map shows all eleven of the Pictish trails featured in this book. The key below explains the notation and abbreviations used in the text.

Reference numbers to stones are prefaced by their Class, I, II or III, and followed by their sequence number given in the book *The Symbol Stones of Scotland*.

Symbols on the stones are given in **bold type**. NB — the sign * denotes symbol 24 or mirror-and-comb.

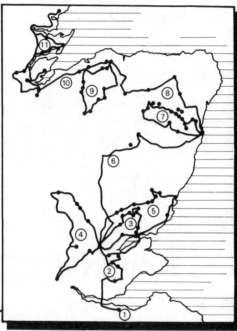

Sign + denotes mirror only.

**Key**

NT National Trust.

SS Secretary of State for Scotland.

❖ Agricultural field. Access is only possible when field is under grass, or after cropping.

✪ Place of historic interest.

Ⓜ Museum

---

 ## TRAIL 1. EDINBURGH:
National Museums of Scotland, Queen Street

---

The following stones may be seen on display if marked with a circle ● (Mon-Sat, 10am-5pm, Sun 2-5pm). Items in store (unmarked) may be seen on prior application to the Assistant Keeper, Archaeology Department (tel: 031 225 7534 ext. 306). Plain reference numbers in brackets refer to the list in *The Symbol Stones of Scotland* (1984). IB numbers are museum references.

▼

| | |
|---|---|
| **Firth** | IB 24 Orkney Class I (4) symbols **17/8** |
| **Greens** | ●IB 203 Orkney Class I (5) symbols **7/8**+ |
| **Birkle Hill** | IB 188 Caithness Class I (10) symbols **7?/15** |
| **Keiss Bay** | ●IB 168 Caithness Class I (11) symbols **41/17**, ogham |
| **Ackergill** | IB 206 Caithness Class I (12) symbols **17** |

▼

| | |
|---|---|
| Latheron | ●IB 183 Caithness Class I (13) symbols **8** |
| Fiscavaig | ●IB 213 Hebrides Class I (34) symbols **5/8** |
| Benbecula | ●IB 37  Hebrides Class I (35) symbols **1/17** |
| Drumbuie 1 | IB 287 Inverness Class I (48) symbols **45/3** |
| Drumbuie 2 | IB 288 Inverness Class 1 (49) symbols **41/6*** |
| Invereen | IB 227 Inverness Class 1 (50) symbols **8/5** |
| Easterton of Roseisle | ●IB 226 Moray Class I (51) symbols **12?/8*//40g/41** |
| Grantown | IB 10  Moray Class I (68) symbols **37/17?** |
| Findlarig | IB 11  Moray Class I (69) symbols **23/8** |
| Huntly 2 | IB 179 Aberdeen Class I (84) symbols **5** |
| Kintore 2 | ●IB 22  Aberdeen Class I (113) symbols **31/5//31+** |
| Kintore 3 | IB 23  Aberdeen Class I (114) symbols **10/21** |
| Edinburgh | ●IB 1  Midlothian Class I (144) symbols **8/5** |
| Brough of Birsay | ●IB 243 Orkney Class II (2−1) symbols **6/8/31/40e** |
| Latheron | ●IB 183 Caithness Class II (2−4) symbols **40e/41,** ogham |
| Tarbat | IB 190 Ross Class II (2−6) symbols **8/21/45/31?** |
| Hilton of Cadboll | ●IB 189 Ross Class II (2−7) symbols **5/8/2?/*** |
| Woodwray | ●IB 202 Angus Class II (2−23) symbols **3/18** |
| Kingoldrum | ●IB 39  Angus Class II (2−26) symbols ***19/9** |
| Monifieth 1 | IB 26  Angus Class II (2−42) symbols **3/5*** |
| Monifieth 2 | ●IB 27  Angus Class II (2−43) symbols **39d/8** |
| Scoonie | ●IB 110 Fife Class II (2−57) symbols **31/?**, ogham |
| Bressay | ●IB 109 Shetland Class III (3−1) horsemen and 2 clerics and oghams |
| Burghead 8 | IB 96  Moray Class III (3−3) armed horseman |
| Monifieth 3 | IB 28  Angus Class III (3−15) horseman |
| Invergowrie 2 | ●IB 229 Angus Class III (3−18) armed horseman |
| Dull | ●IB 58  Perth Class III (3−26) 2 horsemen and 6 warriors |
| Tullibole | IB 99  Kinross Class III (3−31) horseman |
| Abernethy | IB 98  Perth ogham |
| Burrian | GB 1  Orkney ogham |
| Cunningsburgh | IB 114 Shetland ogham |
| Cunningsburgh | IB 115 Shetland ogham |
| Cunningsburgh | IB 182 Shetland ogham |
| Lunnasting | IB 113 Shetland ogham |
| St Ninian's Isle | IB 112 Shetland ogham |
| Whiteness | IB 256 Shetland ogham |

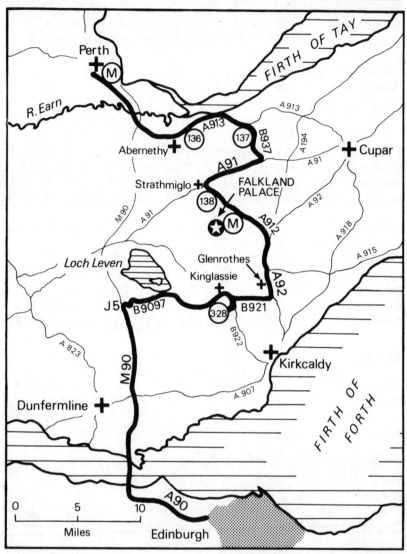

Take the A90 across the Forth Bridge into Fife, where it soon becomes the M90. Leave at Junction 5 to take the B9097, and follow it in the direction of Glenrothes for 7 miles. At Kinglassie, go right down the B922 for a mile, and then turn right to **Dogton Farm**. The stone (3–28) stands 100 yards south of the steading in the stone dyke, and is a Class III monument with an armed horseman. It is protected by railings but is weathering.

32 ▼

Go back to the B9097 and turn right onto the B921. After 3 miles, turn left onto the A92, signposted for Tay Bridge. At Muirhead, take the A912 (signposted for Perth) for Falkland. In **Falkland Palace Museum** Ⓜ there are two Class I stones, (139) and (140), with symbols **6?/22** and **6/3**. The stones have been previously trimmed for use in a wall. (NT, Opening hours: Apr-Oct, weekdays 10am-6pm, Sundays 2-6pm. Nov-Mar, weekends only). **Falkland Palace ⊙** (NT) itself may be of interest. It dates from 1501-1541 and was the favourite seat of James V, (who died here in 1542), and of his daughter, Mary Queen of Scots.
▼

Continue on the A912 to **Strathmiglo**. Turn left into the village, and then immediately left again towards the church. Outside the gates of the **churchyard**, set in the wall, is a Class I stone (138), with symbols **21/39d** on it.
▼

Rejoin the A912 and then turn right onto the A91, heading for St Andrews. Go through Auchtermuchty, then turn left at Collessie up the B937 to Lindores. Here you join the A913 towards Perth, but after 300 yards turn off left to the Grange of **Lindores**. At the church, go left to **Abdie Old Kirk** where you will find the stone in the Mort House by the road. This Class I stone (137) has symbols **4/8+**. Over the years, sadly, it has been used as a sundial and a Grid Reference Point.
▼

Return to the A913, turning left to continue towards Perth. On reaching **Abernethy**, go to the **round tower** in the village. The Class I stone (136) is affixed to the tower. The symbols are **21/8** — note the bold incised work.
▼

From Abernethy, proceed to Perth. There are two stones in the **Perth Museum and Art Gallery** Ⓜ basement, for which prior permission to view should be sought; telephone 0738 32488. (Opening hours: Mon-Sat 10am-1pm, 2-5pm). The Class I stone (135) is from St Madoes and has symbols **3/41//21*//41/44** over three sides, as well as oghams. The Class II stone (2 – 55) has symbols **8/31**.

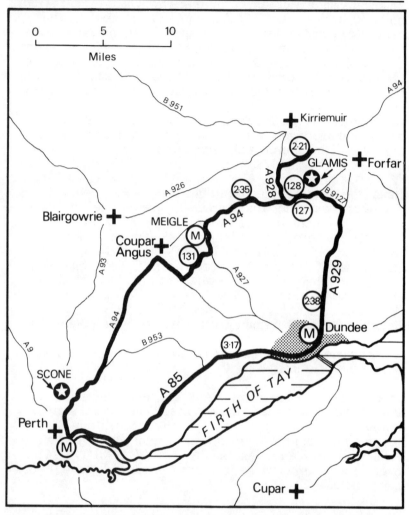

Leave Perth by the A85 for Dundee. Just before the Dundee by-pass, turn off left to Benvie and Fowlis. After ¾ mile, you come to **Benvie old churchyard** on the right. Here, there is a Class III stone (3 – 17) with two armed horsemen in the south-west corner. The stone is covered with lichen and the relief is rather crude.

▼

Go back to the A85 and follow it into **Dundee**, to visit the **McManus Galleries** Ⓜ in Albert Square. (Opening hours: Mon-Sat, 10am-5pm). They have three well-incised Class I stones:

34 ▼

Dunnichen (124) with **46/5\***, Aberlemno 5 (125) with **12/31**, and Strathmartine (132) with **8/31**.

▼

Take the A929 north out of Dundee towards Forfar for 5 miles. At the signpost for the Tealing souterrain and Auchterhouse, turn left to drive west for three miles to **South Balluderon Farm**. You come to the farm just after passing the road to Auchterhouse. In an agricultural field ❖ ½ mile to the south of the farm, and protected by railings, is **St Martin's Stone**, a Class II stone (2 – 38) with **31/45** symbols.

▼

Return to the A929 and continue towards Forfar for 5 miles before turning left onto the B9127 signposted to Douglastown. Turn left again where this road meets the A94, and in 1½ miles (after the signpost to Arniefoul) there is a forest on the left. Pull in when you reach the forest. Walk up the path with the notice "Private, no dogs", for 250 yards only, and the **Glamis 1** stone is on the left in an iron cage. This is a hybrid Class I/II. The Class I side (127) has symbols **37?/44+** while the Class II side (2 – 36) has **4/46**. The symbols are difficult to see as the stone is badly weathered.

▼

Continue a little way on the A94, then turn off right onto the A928 (signposted Kirriemuir) and then right again to **Glamis**. There is another hybrid Class I/II stone in the **manse** garden, next to the church: **Glamis 2** (2 – 37) with **39d/4** on the Class II side and **44/41** on the Class I side (128). This stone is a good example of the hybrid type. Note that in the village there is the **Angus Folk Museum** Ⓜ (NT, Opening hours: May-Sept, 12-5pm). Also note that nearby is **Glamis Castle** ✪ (seat of the Earl of Strathmore and Kinghorne). The castle was the childhood home of Her Majesty Queen Elizabeth The Queen Mother. Malcolm II of Scotland was said to have died there in 1034. The main aspects date from 1675-1687. (May-Sept, 1-5pm except Sat).

▼

Return to the A928 towards Kirriemuir for 1½ miles, then turn right immediately after crossing a railway, following the signpost for Meikle **Cossans**. Follow the road alongside the disused railway track for a mile to the signpost for **St Orland's Stone**. It is a Class II stone (2 – 21) with symbols **8/5** and a horseman. Originally, the defaced central panel may have also contained a horseman.

▼

Go back to the A928, turning back towards Glamis, but then turn right onto the A94 towards Perth. After 2½ miles, turn right to **Eassie** where there is a signpost to the stone. It is in a protective structure in the old **church** and is a Class II stone (2 – 35) with symbols **31/5** which are difficult to see properly.

▼

Proceeding along the A94 towards Perth, turn left at **Meigle** onto the A927 for 200 yards. Turn right, and the **museum** Ⓜ is on the right. (SS, Opening hours: Apr-Sept, Mon-Sat 9.30am-7pm, Oct-Mar, Mon-Sat 9.30am-4pm). The key needs to be fetched: see the noticeboard for details.

▼

> The important stones in the museum are:
> **Meigle 1** (2 – 29) symbols **41/45\* (39b, 31)** plus horsemen
> **Meigle 4** (2 – 30) symbols **31/8** plus horsemen
> **Meigle 5** (2 – 31) symbols **6/31** plus horseman
> **Meigle 6** (2 – 32) symbols **3/9** plus horseman
> **Meigle 7** (2 – 33) symbols **5\***
> **Meigle 2** (3 – 19) horsemen
> **Meigle 3** (3 – 20) horseman
> **Meigle 11** (3 – 21) horsemen
> **Meigle 16** (3 – 22) armed horseman

▼

Continue down the A927 to Newtyle, crossing the railway to turn right for Coupar Angus. After ¾ mile, turn left to Hill of Keillor. In just over a mile, opposite **High Keillor Farm**, there is a Class I stone (131) by the roadside on the right. It is badly weathered but has symbols **38/5 +**.

▼

Carry on along the road until you meet the A923 to Coupar Angus. Turn right. At Coupar Angus, turn left for Perth on the A94.

▼

Note that on the final section of the trail, you pass **Scone Palace** ✪ (seat of the Earl of Mansfield). It was embellished in 1803 and incorporates 16th century and earlier features. The Moot Hill was the site of the famous coronation Stone of Scone brought there in the 9th century by Kenneth mac Alpin, king of the Scots and the Picts. In 1296, the stone was seized by the English and taken to Westminster Abbey — though it is said that this is a copy and that the original is still in Scotland. (Opening hours: Good Friday-mid-Oct, Mon-Sat 10am-5.30pm, Sun 2-5.30pm but Jul-Aug 11am-5.30pm).

# TRAIL 4. PERTH - PITLOCHRY - PERTH
## (125 miles)

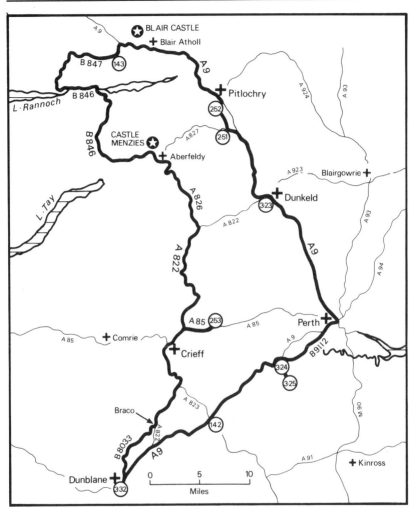

Take the A9 from Perth north to **Dunkeld**. In the **cathedral museum** Ⓜ ✪ there is a Class III stone (3 – 23), **Dunkeld 2**. The detail is difficult to see because of poor lighting, but you should be able to make out the figures of horsemen and several men. (SS, Opening hours: Apr-Sept, Mon-Sat 9.30am-7pm, Sun 2-7pm; Oct-Mar, Mon-Sat 9.30am-4pm, Sun 2-4pm).
▼

Carry on northwards along the A9 and after 8 miles turn off right at Ballinluig onto the A827 for **Logierait**. In 1 mile the church is on the left, and in the **churchyard** there is a Class II
▼

stone (2 – 51) with symbol **45** and a horseman.
▼

Return back along the A827 for 200 yards, then take the narrow minor road to the left, to **Dunfallandy** Catt. After 3½ miles, turn left over a cattle-grid where, near the churchyard, there is a Class II stone (2 – 52). It is enclosed in a glass-plated box and difficult to see, but has symbols **31/?//3/8//8/31**, along with two seated figures and a horseman.
▼

Carry on to Pitlochry and continue on the A9 for 9½ miles, before leaving by the right for the B847 and B846 (signposted Kinloch Rannoch). Note that the road takes you past **Blair Castle** ✪ at Blair Atholl, seat of the Duke of Atholl. The oldest part of the castle is Cumming's Tower, built in 1269. The Duke is the only person allowed to maintain a private army — The Atholl Highlanders. Mary Queen of Scots, Prince Charles Edward and Queen Victoria have all stayed at the castle. (Opening hours: Apr 20th-Oct 12th, Mon-Sat 10am-6pm, Sun 2-6pm). Turn immediately left to Calvine and left again to Struan on the B847. Go past the inn and left for **Old Struan** where, in the church, by the altar, there is a Class I stone (143), with symbols **5/12?**.
▼

Continue on the B847 for 6 miles, then turn left onto the B846 for Tummel Bridge and Aberfeldy, where you take the A826 and A822 towards Crieff. Note that in Aberfeldy you are only 1½ miles from **Castle Menzies** ✪ (Menzies Clan Society). It is a fine example of a 16th century Z-plan fortified tower house. (Opening hours: Apr-Sept, Mon-Sat 10.30am-5pm, Sun 2-5pm). Just before reaching Crieff, turn left at Gilmerton towards Perth, and in 3 miles turn left to **Fowlis Wester**. Here in the village square is a Class II stone (2 – 53) which has symbols **5/8** and three horsemen. The stone is weathered and the figures difficult to see at certain times of the day. The chain on the cross side was probably used for the medieval jougs or pillory. An old custom, maintained up to 1900, was to smear the stone with animal fat once a year.
▼

Return to Gilmerton, then follow the A822 through Crieff and on towards Stirling for 9 miles. At Braco, turn right onto the B8033, (signposted Kinbuck), after which the road joins the A9 to **Dunblane**. There is a Class III stone (3 – 32) inside the **cathedral** ✪ at the west end, depicting an armed horseman. (SS, Apr-Sept, Mon-Sat 9.30am-7pm, Sun 2-5.30pm; Oct-Mar, Mon-Sat 9.30am-4pm, Sun 2-4pm).
▼

Take the A9 north for Perth, looking after about 15 miles for the A823, (signposted Crieff). Leave the A9 on the left, to turn right onto the A823, (signposted Dunfermline). Cross the bridge, and in 50 yards turn right down a disused road. There is the Class I

▼

stone (142) of **Blackford Farm** on the left. It has symbols **40g/?** but is badly weathered.

▼

Rejoin the A9 for 10 miles towards Perth. After Auchterarder, turn right onto the B934 to **Forteviot**. In less than a mile the road forks: B9112 to Perth, and B935 to Forteviot. Go to Forteviot church, where the Class III stone (3–25) is in the vestibule. It is only a fragment and badly weathered but depicts an armed horseman. The key to the church is with the church officer: see the noticeboard.

▼

Return to the fork, to take this time the B9112 for ½ mile. Take the first farm track to the left (unsignposted) to **Bankhead Farm**. Drive round behind the farm steading and continue until the road turns sharp left. Stop and walk on for 100 yards, parallel to the B9112, to find a superb example of a free-standing cross — the **Dupplin** cross, a Class III stone (3–24) depicting a horseman and six warriors.

▼

Go back to the B9112 for Perth.

Aberlemno
stone.
(Trail 5)

# TRAIL 5. PERTH - MONTROSE - PERTH
## (130 miles)

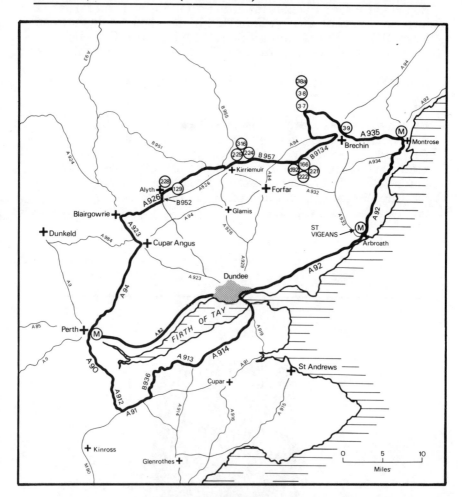

Leave Perth by the A94 for Coupar Angus. At Coupar Angus, turn left onto the A923 for Blairgowrie, where you turn right onto the A926 Kirriemuir road. After 4 miles, turn left onto the B952 to **Alyth**. Head for the parish **church** at the northern end of the town. Here in the vestibule there is a Class II stone (2–28), with a symbol **5** on the back of it. The stone is mounted in a heavy wooden frame, making the symbol difficult to see. If the church is closed, apply to the Beadle; see noticeboard.

▼

Take the B952 out of Alyth towards Glenisla. After 1½ miles turn right onto an unclassified road towards Airlie. After 2

40 ▼

miles, you come to **Bruceton Farm** on the left. The symbol stone (129) is south of the farm between the road and the river in an agricultural field ❖. It has the symbols **12/31**.
▼

Continue on this road to **Kirriemuir**. In the town, take the Brechin road, the B957, and follow the sign for Barrie's birthplace. Carry on along this road for a little, and turn left up Cemetery Road. Climb to the top of the cemetery, where the stones are kept in a wooden shed. Unfortunately, the stones are placed behind glass so that only the sides with the crosses are showing. The stones are **Kirriemuir 1** (2 – 24) with symbol **\*18**, **Kirriemuir 2** (2 – 25) with symbol **5**, and **Kirriemuir 3** (3 – 16) with two armed horsemen.
▼

Continue on the B957 through Tannadice, and go on to meet the A94 at Finavon, going right in the Perth direction for ¾ mile and then turning left (signposted for Bogardo and Finavon Hill) for **Aberlemno**. Turn left when the small road you are on meets the B9134. In the village of Aberlemno, turn right to the **church**, where there is a good example of a Class II stone, **Aberlemno 2** (2 – 21), with the symbols **23/4** and armed horsemen. Returning to the B9134, proceed a few hundred yards. You will find, on the right, a Class II stone, **Aberlemno 3** (2 – 22) with symbols **8/5**, and a Class I stone, **Aberlemno 1** (126) with symbols **44/5\***. There is also a third stone, **Aberlemno 5**, but this has no discernible symbols.
▼

Continue on the B9134 in the direction of Brechin, but on regaining the A94 go left towards Forfar for 3 miles. Turn right for **Menmuir**. After another 3 miles, turn right at the T-junction, and the **church** is shortly on the right. The key is available at the old manse further down the lane. The stones are up in the balcony of the church. They are **Menmuir 1** (3 – 7) and **Menmuir 2** (3 – 8), each of which has a horseman. There is also **Menmuir 3** (3 – 8a) with a horseman. Be prepared for poor lighting.
▼

Carry on along this road, keeping to the right, down to **Brechin**. In the **cathedral** ✪ there is a Class III stone (3 – 9), which has a horseman beneath two seated clerics. The stone, which was originally at Aldbar, is good of its type.
▼

From Brechin, take the A935 to **Montrose**. In the town turn right onto the A92, and after 300 yards, turn left (signposted for the beach), then turn right at Provost Scott's Road and continue for 1200 yards. The **museum** Ⓜ is in Panmure Place, on the right. (Apr-Oct, Mon-Sat 10.30am-1pm, 2-5pm; Jul-Aug also Sun 2-5pm; Nov-Mar, Mon-Fri 2-5pm, Sat 10.30am-1pm, 2-5pm). There are two Class III stones, **Inchbrayock 1** (3 – 10) and **Inchbrayock 2** (3 – 11), each of which has an armed horseman, both weathered.
▼

Return to the A92 and proceed southwards towards Arbroath. Just before reaching the town, turn right for **St Vigeans Museum** Ⓜ (signposted). After 500 yards, turn right, then left where another signpost leads you under a railway bridge. Park and walk over the bridge to the museum. (SS, Apr-Sept, Mon-Sat 9.30am-7pm, Sun 2-7pm; Oct-Mar, Mon-Sat 9.30am-4pm, Sun 2-4pm). The keyholder lives in No. 5 and the key is in a box outside the door. The most interesting stones in St Vigeans Museum are:

▼

| | | |
|---|---|---|
| **St Vigeans 1** | **and 1a** (2 – 44) | symbols **5/9*** |
| **St Vigeans 2** | (2 – 45) | symbols **3?/?//45/40e** |
| **St Vigeans 3** | (2 – 46) | symbols **5** |
| **St Vigeans 4** | (2 – 47) | symbols **3?** |
| **St Vigeans 5** | (2 – 48) | symbols **?/5** |
| **St Vigeans 6** | (2 – 49) | symbols **5** |
| **St Vigeans 17** | (3 – 13) | horseman |
| **St Vigeans 22** | (3 – 14) | armed horseman |

▼

Return to the A92 and follow it to Dundee, there going onto the A85 for Perth. For an alternative and more varied route back to Perth, follow the A92 through Dundee and across the Tay Bridge. Shortly after reaching the Fife side, turn right onto the A914, and subsequently turn right onto the A913, heading for Perth. After Lindores, however, turn left down the B936 for Auchtermuchty, turning right onto the A91. At Gateside, turn right onto the A912 through the Glenfarg pass, and so on to Perth.

Aberlemno 1
stone.
(Trail 5)

# TRAIL 6. PERTH - ABERDEEN
## (110 miles)

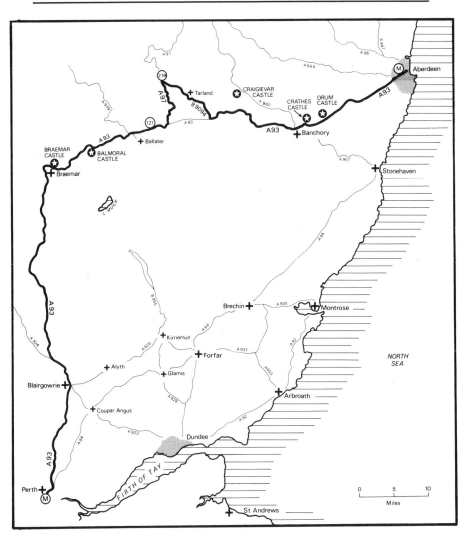

From Perth, take the A93 north to Braemar, travelling through
Blairgowrie and Spittal of Glenshee, then round the Devil's
Elbow. You may want to take the opportunity to visit **Braemar
Castle ✪** (seat of Farquharson of Invercauld). It was built in
1628 by the Earl of Mar, burnt by Farquharson in 1689, then
rebuilt in 1748. (Opening hours: May-Oct, daily 10am-6pm).

Follow the A93 towards Ballater, passing **Balmoral Castle ✪**
(owned by H.M. The Queen). This has been a Royal Family

▼

43

Home for over a century. It dates back to 1484, but it was rebuilt by Prince Albert and first occupied in 1855. (Gardens open May-Jul, Mon-Sat 10am-5pm). Two miles beyond Ballater, on the right, is **Tullich church**. Against the north wall of the ruined church in a railed enclosure is a Class I stone (121) which is badly weathered but has symbols **5/31\***.

▼

Continue on the A93 for a couple of miles, then turn left onto the A97 (signposted Huntly). Continue for 2½ miles, then turn left for Roebush and regain the A97. After ½ mile, turn right to **Migvie**. In another mile, keep left at the fork (no signpost). The **church** is on the right, further west. There is a Class II stone (2 – 19) just inside the churchyard. It is weathered, but you should be able to see two symbols, **5** and **13**, as well as a horseman.

▼

Return past Meadow Farm on the small road to Tarland, turning right onto the A974, then in half a mile turn left onto the B9094 to Aboyne. At Aboyne, turn left onto the A93 for Aberdeen.

▼

An alternative route from Tarland to Aberdeen is obtained by turning left in Tarland onto the A974, instead of right. After 5 miles, turn left up the A980 for 2 miles to **Craigievar Castle ✪**. This fairytale castle was completed in 1626 for William Forbes and has been untouched ever since. (NT, May-Sept, 2-6pm).

Go back down the A980 and follow it to Banchory, turning left there to rejoin the A93 for Aberdeen. Note that just past Banchory is **Crathes Castle ✪**. It dates from 1533 and is an outstanding example of a Scottish tower. (NT, May-Sept, Mon-Sat 11am-6pm, Sun 2-6pm). Four miles further along the A93, to the left, is **Drum Castle ✪**. The earliest part of the castle is 13th century and adjoins a mansion of 1619. (NT, May-Sept, 2-6pm).

▼

In Aberdeen visit the **University Anthropological Museum ⓜ** Marischal College (Mon-Fri 10am-5pm, Sun 2-5pm). It has three Class I stones: **Tillytarmont 1** (78) with symbols **40g/6\***, **Wantonwells** (89b) with symbol **5**, and **Collace** (133) with symbols **?/31\***. (In the entrance to the Grampian Region Headquarters in West Burn Road, Aberdeen, there is a stone with a Pictish warrior. It is not a symbol stone, but may be of interest).

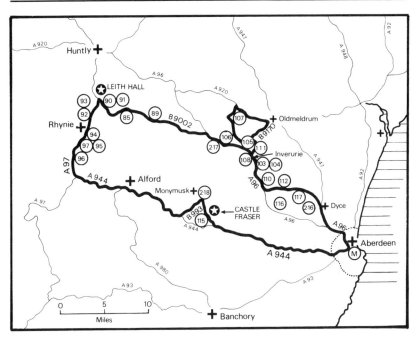

Leave Aberdeen by the A96, soon going onto the A947 to **Dyce**.
In the middle of the village, opposite the parish church, turn left
along the Pitmedden road. After ¾ mile, turn left under the
railway, (signposted Kinaldie), and after ½ mile the signpost,
"Pictish Symbol Stones", leads to the **old chapel**. On the east
wall are the two stones. The Class I stone (117) has symbols
**31/5**, and the Class II stone (2 – 16) has symbols **8/4 −6/5**.
▼

Continue on the small lane westwards for 3 miles, then turn left
(signposted Blackburn). After ½ mile, turn right (no signpost), cross
the river and the B979, then take the lane for Kirkton. After 3¾
mile you reach **Kinellar church**. Inside the porch, on a wall, is a
Class I stone (116) with symbols **1/8**. Be prepared for poor lighting.
▼

Carry on along this small road for 2½ miles to **Kintore**. On the
right, at the entrance to the church, there is a Class I stone
(112). It is engraved on both sides, and the symbols are
**41/4//8/31**.
▼

From Kintore, take the A96 in the Inverness direction. The road
passes the paper-mill, then, before Port Elphinstone, there is a
stone circle on the right, near **Crichie**. Stop near the drive
▼

45

signposted Broom Lodge. There is a Class I stone (110) with symbols **31/8**, standing in an agricultural field ❖ to the left of the drive.
▼

Continue towards **Inverurie**, shortly turning right onto the B993 towards Whiterashes. The **cemetery** is just after the railway bridge. Here, to the left under some trees, are two Class I stones: **Inverurie 1** (103) with symbols **8/6/45/5**, and **Inverurie 3** (104) with symbols **?/5**. They may be difficult to see.
▼

Return to Inverurie along the A96. In the village, turn right onto the B9170 for Old Meldrum. After 4 miles, turn right for Kirkton of **Bourtie**. A class I stone (111) is built into the outside of the **church**, high up at the west end of the south face. Because of the height of the stone, the only way to make out the symbols is to use binoculars! They are, in fact, **8/5\***.
▼

Go back to Inverurie and take the A96 north. On the outskirts of the village, to the left, there is **Brandsbutt Farm**. The Class I stone, Brandsbutt (108), with symbols **8/45** and an ogham, is signposted. The stone is a good example of Class I, and also of what can happen to Pictish symbol stones over the years. At one stage it was broken up to be put in a dyke. Once in a field, it is now in the middle of a new housing estate.
▼

Return to the A96 and cross it to join the B9001. After a mile, turn left to **East Balhalgardy Farm** where there is a Class I stone (105) in the top lintel of a window in the old steading to the left of the farm track. This stone is weathered as well as recycled. The symbol is **5**.
▼

Continue left along this small road, past the Battle of Harlaw monument, and, bearing left, rejoin the A96, following it for 1 mile. At the entrance to **Drimmies Farm**, by the road on the left-hand side, is a Class I stone (106) with symbols **12/14\***.
▼

Take the small road (signposted Chapel of Garioch) opposite Drimmies Farm, and go past Chapel of Garioch. In a mile, on the left, there is the **Maiden Stone**. It is a Class II stone (2 – 17), one of the few in Aberdeenshire but an excellent example of the class. It has symbols **23/31\***.
▼

Continue on the small road, then turn left to rejoin the A96 and then take the B9002, to Insch. In the village of Insch take the B992, turning right towards Auchterless. In less than a mile go left to Largie (signposted for the **Picardy Stone**). After 1½ miles, look out on the left for the Class I stone (89). There is no marker for it, but once you have found it you will see it is a nice stone, somewhat weathered, with the symbols **5/45\***.
▼

Carry on along the lane, and then bear right at the T-junction. After ½ mile, turn left (signposted Wardhouse). In less than a mile, bear left at Weets Farm and then fork right to rejoin the B9002. Turn right for Kennethmont Halt. After passing the distillery take the first left turn. Drive 1 mile to **Ardlair Farm**. South of this is a Class I stone (85) which has symbols **31/21+**.
▼

Go back to the B9002. In 1 mile, turn right to **Leith Hall ⊘** (signposted). This has been the home of the Leith family since 1650. (NT, May-Sept, 2-6pm). At the top of the garden (open all the year), in a shed, are two Class I stones, both weathered. **Newbigging Leslie** (90) has symbols **17/38***, and **Percylieu** (91) has symbols **41/12**.
▼

Return towards Kennethmont, but in 500 yards turn right to **Rhynie**. You now rejoin the A97, turning left onto it. In Rhynie there is a Class I stone (92) on the village green, but weathered to the point that nothing much can be seen on it anymore.
▼

In Rhynie turn left for Clatt. Cross the Water of Bogie, and in ½ mile turn right for **Barflat Farm** where there is a Class I stone (97) with symbols **31/?** outside the farmhouse.
▼

Return to Rhynie and turn left. In 100 yards, turn left again (signposted (Rhynie cemetery). At the entrance to the **old graveyard** there are two Class I stones, badly weathered: **Rhynie 5** (94) with symbols **39b/5*** and **Rhynie 6** (95) with symbols **5/8+**.
▼

Go back to the A97 and proceed south for ½ mile to the Mains of Rhynie farm road. In an agricultural field ❖ to the left is the **Craw Stone**. It is **Rhynie 1** (96) with symbols **41/31**. Note the superb position of the stone, and its relation to the nearby stones.
▼

Continue down the A97 for 4 miles. Take the left fork to Aberdeen, going onto the A944 and following it for 11 miles. Then take the B933 towards Kemnay. In 3 miles, stop at **Monymusk**. In the **church** there is a Class II stone (2 – 18) which has symbols **19/4**.
▼

Carry on along the B993 and turn left. After 2 miles, turn right for Craigearn, then right again for **Castle Fraser ⊘**. This was begun in 1575 and completed in 1636. (NT, May-Sept, 2-6pm). Continue to **Dunecht**. The symbol stone is in a field to the south. It is **Nether Corskie** (115), a Class I stone with the symbol **6***.
▼

Go back to the A944 and follow it to Aberdeen. This trail can be made in one day, but you might like to spend two days on it.

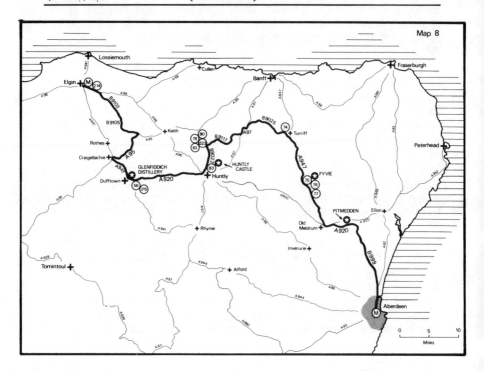

Take the A92 out of Aberdeen, going north for Peterhead. Just over a mile beyond Bridge of Don turn left onto the B999 to Pitmedden. Here is **Pitmedden Garden** ✪ — a 17th century Great Garden. (NT, 9.30am-sunset).

Take the B9000 west into Old Meldrum, and there turn right onto the A947 to **Fyvie**. Turn right into the village, then bear right for the **church**. Built into the wall of the church there are three Class I stones (75–77): **Rothiebrisbane** with **12/1** symbols, **Fyvie 1** with **8/31+**, and **Fyvie 2** with **3/40e**. Note that there is a castle at **Fyvie** which dates back to the 13th century but displays five centuries of Scottish history. (NT, May-Sept, 2-6pm).

▼

Go back onto the A947 and keep following it north to Turriff. There, go left onto the B9024, until at its T-junction with the A97, turn left for **Huntly**. In the middle of the town square is a Class I stone (83) with a barely distinguishable symbol **12** on it. You will see from the position of the stone why it is deteriorating. Note that there is a ruined castle in **Huntly** ✪ which was once owned by the Gay Gordons. (SS, Apr-Sept, Mon-Sat 9.30am-7pm, Sun 2-7pm; Oct-Mar, Mon-Sat 9.30am-4pm, Sun 2-4pm).

▼

Take the B9014 westwards out of Huntly to Dufftown. In the town go left at Mortlach distillery to **Kirkton of Mortlach** (signposted Mortlach cemetery). A Class I stone (56) is in the vestibule of the church. It is difficult to view and poorly lit, but has the symbols **31/?**. In the lower graveyard extension is a weathered Class II stone (2 – 15) with symbols **43 – 43//40e/44** and a horseman.

▼

Return to Dufftown and take the A941 to Craigellachie. There turn right onto the A95 towards Keith, following the road for 6 miles. At the edge of the forest, turn left onto the B9013 to Elgin. After 2 miles on this road, it crosses the River Spey. Just after this turn right at the T-junction (unsignposted) to keep on the B9013. Keep following the road until it meets the A96 outside Elgin. Visit the **Elgin Museum** Ⓜ As well as examples of the Burghead bull, it has one Class I stone (52), **Drainie**, with symbol **8**. There are also two Class III stones: **Drainie 3** (3 – 4) with a horseman, and **Drainie 13** (3 – 5) with two horsemen and five men. Also visit **Elgin Cathedral** ✪ (SS, Apr-Sept, Mon-Sat 9.30am-7pm, Sun 2-7pm; Oct-Mar, Mon-Sat 9.30am-4pm, Sun 2-4pm). In the grounds there is a Class II stone (2 – 14). It is a rare but good example of a Class II stone in granite, and has symbols **5/8** and four horsemen.

Detail of Dunfallandy Stone. (Trail 4)

# TRAIL 9. ELGIN - GRANTOWN-ON-SPEY - ELGIN
## (65 miles)

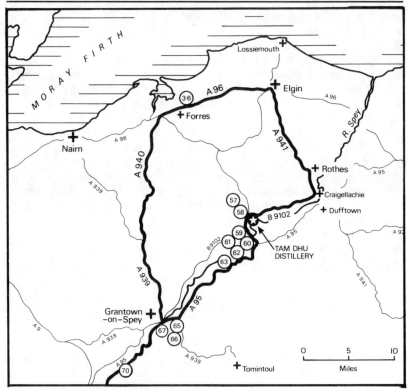

Leave Elgin by the main road south; the A941 signposted Perth. Follow the road to Craigellachie, where you turn right onto the B9102 (signposted Knockando) and go to **Upper Knockando**. Here turn right (signposted Knockando school and churchyard), then at the school turn left for the church. Built into the wall at the **churchyard** entrance are two Class I stones: **Knockando 1** (57) with symbols **1?/8/8**, and **Knockando 2** (58) with symbols **44/?+**. Note that nearby is the **Tamdhu Distillery** (Opening hours: Easter-Sept 30th, Mon-Sat 10am-4pm).

▼

Continue on the B9102 for 3 miles, then turn left on the B9131 (signposted Marypark). Cross the river and turn right onto the A95 (signposted Grantown). After 1 mile, turn right to **Inveravon church**. Four Class I stones have been mounted against the south wall of the church. All are weathering fast. **Inveravon 1** (62) has symbols **6/40e***, **Inveravon 2** (61) has **8/4***, **Inveravon 3** (60) has **31**, and **Inveravon 4** (59) has **8/31**.

▼

Return to the A95, and continue for 6 miles to **Advie church**, on the right. Set in the north wall of the sacristy is a Class I stone (63). It is badly weathered but has symbols **8/6**.

▼

Continuing on the A95 for 7 miles, you come to **Congash Farm** on the left. Ask permission to park at the farm and go through the steading, diagonally opposite the farmhouse. Follow the path across the field, and at the drainage dyke go south into the next field and towards the top for 200 yards. There is a large circular cairn in the field, and on either side of its "entrance" at the south there are two Class I stones. They are sunk in the ground and the symbols are hard to see, but you should look at **Congash 1** (65) for symbols **12/31**, and at **Congash 2** (66) for symbols **5/11**.

▼

Go back to the A95, and continue in the direction of Grantown-on-Spey. Cross the River Spey into the town, then turn left (signposted Perth) to keep on the A95. After 100 yards, go left towards **Inverallan old kirkyard**, travelling along by the river. Set in the kirkyard wall facing the river is a Class I stone (67), badly weathered but with symbols **8/23**.

▼

Continue on the A95 for 3 miles, and turn left to cross the river towards Nethy Bridge. Turn right down the B970 for 6 miles to Kincardine churchyard. Here is a Class I stone (70): **Lynchurn** with symbol **8**.

▼

Return to Grantown-on-Spey, and turn left onto the A939 heading north towards Nairn. At Dava take the right-hand fork, the A940, for **Forres**. At the end of the town, turn left onto the B9011. Almost immediately, there is **Sueno's Stone** on the left. This is a magnificent stone and worth studying carefully. It is a Class III stone (3–6) and is covered with figures, but is weathering rapidly.

▼

Return to the A96, turn left onto it and follow it back to Elgin.

# TRAIL 10. ELGIN - INVERNESS
## (65 miles)

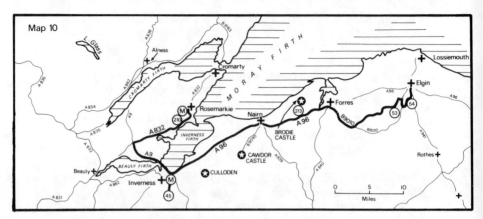

Set off south from Elgin on the A941 (signposted Perth). ¾ mile after the railway crossing, turn right down a small road signposted Birnie and bearing right. After 1½ miles, there is **Birnie church** on the left. By the kirkyard wall, on the right, there is a Class I stone (54) which has symbols **40e/23**. It is badly weathered.
▼

Continue on this road for ½ mile, and then turn right onto the B9010. After 500 yards, take a left turn at **Easter Manbeen Farm**. Two more left turns take you to **Upper Manbeen Farm**. In an agricultural field ❖ to the west stands a Class I stone (53) that has symbols **39b/41***. This stone is badly weathered but is one of the very few stones where symbols are placed horizontally and not vertically.
▼

Returning to the minor road that you left at Easter Manbeen Farm, turn left to continue towards Forres. After about 1½ miles, turn left at the T-junction and carry on until you reach the B9010, heading for Forres. On the way to Forres, you will pass **Pluscarden Abbey ✪** which was founded in 1230. It became Benedictine in 1454 but was suppressed in 1560. It was refounded in 1948.

At Forres, turn left along the A96, and after 3 miles, turn right towards **Brodie Castle ✪** which was rebuilt from an earlier structure (NT, Opening hours: May 1st-Oct 31st, Mon-Sat 10am-6pm, Sun 2-6pm). At a road junction is **Rodney's Stone**. It is a Class II stone (2 – 13) with symbols **43 – 43//31/5**, as well as oghams.
▼

After Brodie, you can either follow the main A96 through Nairn to Inverness, or else turn off at Auldearn onto an alternative route to visit two further places of interest. To do this, you turn

▼

onto the B9101 at Auldearn. After about 2 miles, the road crosses the A939 and becomes the B9090, taking you to Cawdor and **Cawdor Castle** ✪ (seat of the Earl of Cawdor). This is a central tower of 1372, rebuilt in 1454, surrounded by a 16th century building. It has been a family home for over 600 years (Opening hours: May 1st-Oct 5th, daily 10am-5.30pm).

About 1 mile after Cawdor, turn left onto the B9101 to Croy, then left onto the B9006 to go past the battlefield of **Culloden** ✪. Here, Prince Charles Edwards's army was crushed by King George's troops on 16th April, 1746, in 40 minutes. There are memorial cairns to the 1,200 Highlanders who died. The road joins the A9 just before Inverness.

▼

In Inverness, there are four Class I stones in **Inverness Museum** ⓜ in Castle Wynd (Opening hours: Mon-Sat, 9am-5pm). Check beforehand that the stones are on display, as they are rotated between the gallery and the store). The stones are **Torgorm** (42) with symbols **5/5**, **Wester Balblair** (43) with **15/8**, **Garbeg** (44) with **8/?**, and **Cullaird** (47) with **23/12***.

▼

At the Town Hall, turn onto the A861 going south from Inverness (signposted Culduthel). Follow the road for 2 miles, then turn right for Essich. After ¾ mile, you come to a T-junction where you turn left for Essich. After ½ mile, on the left, is the **Boar Stone**. It is a Class I stone (45) with symbols **6/34**. It is covered with wire mesh, and the symbols are practically impossible to make out.

▼

Return north to Inverness, and take the new A9 road over the Kessock Bridge. At the Tore roundabout, turn right onto the A832 for **Rosemarkie**. After 2 miles there is a "cloutie well", or wishing-well, on the right. In the little **Groam House Museum** ⓜ in Rosemarkie is an excellent Class II stone (2 – 10) which has the symbols **8/8//5/8+ +**. (Opening hours: Mon-Sat, 10.30am-12.30pm, 2.30-4.30pm, Sun 2.30-4.30pm).

▼

Return to the Tore roundabout, and follow the A9 back to Inverness.

Rosemarkie stone.
(Trail 10)

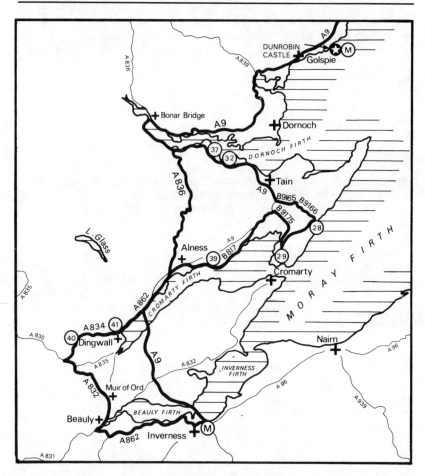

From Inverness, take the A862 around the Beauly Firth, and at
Muir of Ord turn left onto the A832 towards Ullapool. At Contin,
turn right onto the A834 for **Strathpeffer**. In the middle of the
village of Strathpeffer, follow the sign for the **Eagle Stone**
(opposite the Ben Wyvis Hotel). This is a Class I stone (40) with
symbols **12/40e**.
▼

Carry on along the A834 to **Dingwall**. Go left at the by-pass,
cross the railway and turn right for the town centre and the
parish **church** on the right. To the left of the entrance path to
the church there is a Class I stone (41), badly weathered, with
symbols **5/8/8//1?/8**.

54    ▼

Return to the by-pass, turn right and continue on the A862 towards Alness until it joins the A9. Before Alness, turn left onto the A836 (signposted Bonar Bridge). Follow this road until it joins the A9 before Bonar Bridge. Carry on up the A9 through Golspie, and then turn right into **Dunrobin Castle** ✪ (seat of the Countess of Sutherland). Based on a keep built in 1275, this magnificent building, rebuilt in 1845-1850, has been the seats of the Earls and Dukes of Sutherland for centuries. (Opening hours: June 1st-Sept 15th, Mon-Sat 10.30am-5.30pm, Sun 1-5.30pm). The journey north to Dunrobin is a long one, so you should check in advance that the castle and museum are open. (telephone 04083-3177). The castle **museum** Ⓜ contains:

▼

| | | |
|---|---|---|
| Navidale | (14) Class I with symbols | 4? |
| Kintradwell 2 | (16) Class I with symbols | 14+ |
| Kintradwell 1 | (17) Class I with symbols | 14/7 |
| Kintradwell 4 | (18) Class I with symbols | 21? |
| Kintradwell 3 | (19) Class I with symbols | 8* |
| Clynemilton 1 | (20) Class I with symbols | 12/8+ |
| Clynemilton 2 | (21) Class I with symbols | 23* |
| Clynekirkton 2 | (22) Class I with symbols | 17/8+ |
| Clynekirkton 1 | (23) Class I with symbols | 8/17 |
| Dunrobin | (24) Class I with symbols | 41/21* |
| Golspie 2 | (25) Class I with symbols | 8/31* |
| Golspie 3 | (26) Class I with symbols | 10/45* |
| Little Ferry Links 4 | (27) Class I with symbols | 8? |
| Little Ferry Links 1 | (28) Class I with symbols | 17? |
| Little Ferry Links 2 | (29) Class I with symbols | 12/8? |
| Craigton | (30) Class I with symbols | 21/8/46 |
| Golspie | (2–5) Class II with symbols | 17/31//35d/41 //46/8//3/44 and ogham |

▼

From Dunrobin, go back south down the A9, following the road round the Dornoch Firth rather than going back over Struie Hill on the A836. About 5 miles beyond this junction, turn left to **Edderton village**. On the immediate left there is a Class I stone (37) in an agricultural field ❖. It is badly weathered and has symbols **41/5**.

▼

Continue along the A9, and ¾ miles later you come to **Edderton old cemetery** on the left. Here, there is a Class III stone (3–2) with three horsemen. Two of the horsemen are difficult to see. The stone also has crosses on both sides.

▼

Carry on along the A9, then 2½ miles past the Tain turning, go left onto the B9165 for Fearn. Then take the B9166 to Balintore.

▼

Turn south to **Shandwick** and continue up the hill, to find a Class II stone (2–8) on the right in an agricultural field ❖. It is badly weathered but has symbols **3/31** and three horsemen.

▼

Continue on this road, and go left for **Nigg village**. After 2 miles you will reach **Nigg church** on the right. Inside the church is a magnificent Class II stone (2–9) with symbols **40e/31** and a horseman.

▼

Go back north up the B9175, to the T-junction with the A9, where you turn left for Dingwall and **Invergordon**. Just over 2 miles along the A9, turn left along the B817 (signposted "alternative route to Invergordon"). Half a mile after the village and just before a signpost on the left to a public slipway, is the **Roskeen stone**. It is on the right in an agricultural field ❖. It is a Class I stone (39), with symbols **19?/8?/21?**, and is used as a cattle rubbing post.

▼

Take the A9 back to Inverness.

▼

From Inverness, it takes little more than three hours to return down the A9 to Edinburgh. Alternatively, you can take the slower but attractive roads along Loch Ness to Fort Augustus and Spean Bridge. From here, the A86 goes towards Kingussie, and the possibility of a further small detour round Laggan on the A86 and the A889 before rejoining the A9 at Dalwhinnie.

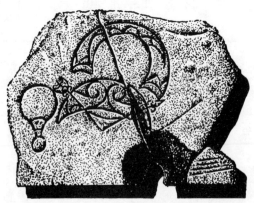

Clynemilton 1
stone.
(Trail 11)

# STONES TOO DISTANT OR TOO PRIVATE TO VISIT ON THESE TRAILS

## Class I:

| | | |
|---|---|---|
| (3) | Orkney, | Knowe of Burrian. Tankerness House Museum. |
| (8) | Caithness, | Sandside House (private). |
| (31) | Ross, | Gairloch. Gairloch Museum. |
| (32) | Skye, | Snizort. |
| (33) | Skye, | Dunvegan. Dunvegan Castle Museum. |
| (36) | Western Isles, | Pabbay. |
| (46) | Inverness, | Essich House. Stoneyfield House (private). |
| (55) | Banff, | Arndilly House (private). |
| (71) | Aberdeen, | Tyrie. Inside church. |
| (72) | Aberdeen, | Fetterangus. In churchyard. |
| (79) | Aberdeen, | Tillytarmont 2. Whitestones (private). |
| (80) | Aberdeen, | Tillytarmont 3. Whitestones (private). |
| (81) | Aberdeen, | Tillytarmont 4. Whitehills (private). |
| (82) | Aberdeen, | Tillytarmont 5. Whitehills (private). |
| (82b) | Aberdeen, | Tillytarmont 6. Whitehills (private). |
| (86) | Aberdeen, | Clatt 1. Knockespock House (private). |
| (98) | Aberdeen, | Newton House (private). |
| (100) | Aberdeen, | Logie Elphinstone (private). |
| (101) | Aberdeen, | Logie Elphinstone (private). |
| (102) | Aberdeen, | Logie Elphinstone (private). |
| (107) | Aberdeen, | Daviot. Mounie Castle (private). |
| (109) | Aberdeen, | Keith Hall (private). |
| (118) | Aberdeen, | Park House (private). |
| (119) | Aberdeen, | Craigmyle House (private). |
| (120) | Aberdeen, | Mar Coldstone. Tillypronie House (private). |
| (123) | Angus, | Inverkeillor. Kinblethmont House (private). |
| (141) | Fife, | Walton. Crawford Priory (private). |

## Class II:

| | | |
|---|---|---|
| (2) | Caithness, | Halkirk. Thurso Museum. |
| (3) | Caithness, | Ulbster. Thurso Museum. |
| (11) | Skye, | Raasay, Near Raasay House. |
| (12) | Nairn, | Glenferness (private). |
| (20) | Kincardine, | Fordoun. In church. |
| (34) | Perth, | Rossie Priory (private). |
| (54) | Perth, | Gask House. Moncrieff House (private). |
| (56) | Fife, | Upper Largo. In churchyard. |

## Class III:

| | | |
|---|---|---|
| (27) | Fife, | Mugdrum (private). |
| (29) | Fife, | Sauchope. Crail, Victoria Park. |

Of these 37 stones, 13 may be freely visited but they are remote from our trails. The rest are in private hands. Museums are normally standard hours, but they should be checked beforehand with the local Tourist Board, particularly in winter months.

# LIST OF CLASS I STONES

## Explanation of notation

/ = pair (as in, say, 17/12). // = symbols on both sides of a stone (as, say, 41/4//8/31).
− = symbols are side by side on a stone (as, say, 6 – 23).
+ = mirror. * = mirror and comb.
★ = damaged stone. △ = illegible symbol. §= symbol on pillar. H = ogham present

| | County | Name | Symbol | | Present location | Grid reference of original site |
|---|---|---|---|---|---|---|
| 1 | Shetland | Sandness | 17/12+ | | lost | HU 1912 5765 |
| 2 | Orkney | Broch of Oxtro | 40e | | lost | HY 2537 2678 |
| 3 | Orkney | Knowe of Burrian | 40e/8+ | | Kirkwall | HY 308 168 |
| 4 | Orkney | Redland, Firth | 17/8 | ★ | Edinburgh | HY 378 171 |
| 5 | Orkney | Greens, St Andrews | 7/8+ | | Edinburgh | HY 542 031 |
| 6 | Orkney | St Peter's, Burwick | 17/8//8/7 | ★ | Edinburgh | ND 4707 9084 |
| 7 | Sutherland | Kirtomy, near Farr | 44? or 45? | ★ | lost | NC 74 63 |
| 8 | Caithness | Sandside House | 15/7* | | private | NC 9522 6518 |
| 9 | Caithness | Thurso Castle | 8/12 | | lost | ND 025 701 |
| 9b | Caithness | Watenan | 8 | | Wick | ND 311 407 |
| 10 | Caithness | Birkle Hill, Keiss | 7?/15 | ★ | Edinburgh | ND 339 584 |
| 11 | Caithness | Keiss Bay | 41/17 | H ★ | Edinburgh | ND 3483 5499 |
| 12 | Caithness | Ackergill | 17 | | Edinburgh | ND 349 550 |
| 13 | Caithness | Latheron | 8 | ★ | lost | ND 1990 3343 |
| 14 | Sutherland | Navidale | 4? | ★ | Dunrobin Castle | ND 0419 1615 |
| 15 | Sutherland | Langdale | 12? | ★ | lost | NC 69 44 |
| 16 | Sutherland | Kintradwell 2 | 14+ | ★ | Dunrobin Castle | NC 9283 0806 |
| 17 | Sutherland | Kintradwell 1 | 14/7 | ★ | Dunrobin Castle | NC 9283 0806 |
| 18 | Sutherland | Kintradwell 4 | 21? | ★ | Dunrobin Castle | NC 9316 0838 |
| 19 | Sutherland | Kintradwell 3 | 8* | ★ | Dunrobin Castle | NC 9316 0838 |
| 20 | Sutherland | Clynemilton 1 | 12/8+ | | Dunrobin Castle | NC 914 069 |
| 21 | Sutherland | Clynemilton 2 | 23* | ★ | Dunrobin Castle | NC 914 069 |
| 22 | Sutherland | Clynekirkton 2 | 17/8+ | ★ | Dunrobin Castle | NC 894 060 |
| 23 | Sutherland | Clynekirkton 1 | 8/17 | | Dunrobin Castle | NC 894 060 |
| 24 | Sutherland | Dunrobin Castle | 41/21* | | Dunrobin Castle | NC 8494 0057 |
| 25 | Sutherland | Golspie 2 | 8/31* | | Dunrobin Castle | NC 8338 0018 |
| 26 | Sutherland | Golspie 3 | 10/45* | | Dunrobin Castle | NC 847 003 |
| 27 | Sutherland | Little Ferry Links 4 | 8? | ★ | Dunrobin Castle | NH 814 966 |
| 28 | Sutherland | Little Ferry Links 1 | 17? | ★ | Dunrobin Castle | NH 814 966 |
| 29 | Sutherland | Little Ferry Links 2 | 12/8? | ★ | Dunrobin Castle | NH 814 966 |
| 30 | Sutherland | Craigton | 21/8/46 | § | Dunrobin Castle | NH 8513 0093 |
| 31 | Ross | Gairloch | 40e/41 | ★ | | NG 799 772 |
| 32 | Western Isles | Snizort | 8/5* | | Tote | NG 421 491 |
| 33 | Western Isles | Dunvegan | 8/1 | | | NG 2408 4648 |
| 34 | Western Isles | Fiscavaig | 5/8 | | Edinburgh | NG 330 340 |
| 35 | Western Isles | Benbecula | 1/17 | | Edinburgh | NF 803 566 |
| 36 | Western Isles | Pabbay | 8/46 | | | NL 607 875 |
| 37 | Ross | Edderton | 41/5 | § ★ | | NH 7082 8507 |
| 38 | Ross | Nonakiln | 3/3? | | lost | NH 663 712 |
| 39 | Ross | Roskeen | 19?//8?/21? | § | | NH 681 690 |
| 40 | Ross | Strathpeffer | 12/40e | ★ | | NH 485 585 |
| 41 | Ross | Dingwall | 5/8/8//1?/8 | ★ | | NH 549 589 |
| 42 | Ross | Torgorm | 5/5 | ★ | Inverness | NH 559 549 |
| 43 | Inverness | Wester Balblair | 15/8 | | Inverness | NH 5101 4528 |

| County | Name | Symbol | | Present location | Grid reference of original site |
|---|---|---|---|---|---|
| Inverness | Garbeg, Drumnadrochit | 8/? | ✩ | Inverness | NH 5110 3226 |
| Inverness | Knocknagael | 6/34 | § | | NH 6567 4134 |
| Inverness | Essich House | 34?/3? | ✩ | private | NH 647 395 |
| Inverness | Cullaird, Dores | 23/12* | ✩ | Inverness | NH 6341 4041 |
| Inverness | Drumbuie 1 | 45/3 | ✩ | Edinburgh | NH 510 310 |
| Inverness | Drumbuie 2 | 41/6* | | Edinburgh | NH 510 310 |
| Inverness | Invereen | 8/5 | | Edinburgh | NH 7968 3108 |
| Moray | Easterton of Roseisle | 12?/8*//40g/41 | | Edinburgh | NJ 144 647 |
| Moray | Drainie | 8 | ✩ | Elgin | NJ 223 696 |
| Moray | Upper Manbeen | 39b/41* | | | NJ 1868 5761 |
| Moray | Birnie | 40e/23 | | | NJ 2063 5872 |
| Banff | Arndilly | 6–23 | | private | NJ 2905 4711 |
| Banff | Mortlach | 31/? | | | NJ 323 392 |
| Moray | Knockando 1 | 1?/8/8 | | Knockando Church | NJ 2026 4218 |
| Moray | Knockando 2 | 44/?+ | § | Knockando Church | NJ 2026 4218 |
| Banff | Inveravon 4 | 8/31 | | | NJ 183 376 |
| Banff | Inveravon 3 | 31 | ✩ | | NJ 183 376 |
| Banff | Inveravon 2 | 8/4* | | | NJ 183 376 |
| Banff | Inveravon 1 | 6/40e* | § | | NJ 183 376 |
| Inverness | Advie | 8/6 | ✩ | | NJ 1265 3426 |
| Moray | Balneilean | 1 | | lost | NJ 149 259 |
| Inverness | Congash 1 | 12/31 | | on right-hand jamb | NJ 058 262 |
| Inverness | Congash 2 | 5/11 | | on left-hand jamb | NJ 058 262 |
| Moray | Inverallan | 8/23 | ✩ | | NJ 026 260 |
| Moray | Grantown | 37/17? | | Edinburgh | NJ 0452 3012 |
| Moray | Findlarig | 23/8 | | Edinburgh | NH 991 253 |
| Inverness | Lynchurn | 8 | ✩ | Kincardine Church | NH 953 206 |
| Aberdeen | Tyrie | 40e/23 | | | NJ 930 631 |
| Aberdeen | Fetterangus | ?/6/4 | △ | | NJ 9814 5056 |
| Aberdeen | Old Deer | 17/8 | | lost | NJ 969 481 |
| Aberdeen | Turriff | 5 | ✩ | lost | NJ 7230 4991 |
| Aberdeen | Rothiebrisbane | 12/1 | | Fyvie Church | NJ 745 378 |
| Aberdeen | Fyvie 1 | 8/31+ | ✩ | Fyvie Church | NJ 7688 3777 |
| Aberdeen | Fyvie 2 | 3/40e | ✩ | Fyvie Church | NJ 7688 3777 |
| Aberdeen | Tillytarmont 1 | 40g/6+ | | Aberdeen | NJ 529 464 |
| Aberdeen | Tillytarmont 2 | 8/5 | | Whitestones (private) | NJ 5331 4715 |
| Aberdeen | Tillytarmont 3 | 9/1 | | Whitestones (private) | NJ 533 473 |
| Aberdeen | Tillytarmont 4 | 40e/31 | | Whitehills (private) | NJ 5331 4724 |
| Aberdeen | Tillytarmont 5 | 45/12* | | Whitehills (private) | NJ 5331 4716 |
| Aberdeen | Tillytarmont 6 | 41/5 | | Whitehills (private) | NJ 5331 4716 |
| Aberdeen | Huntly 1 | 12 | §△✩ | | NJ 529 400 |
| Aberdeen | Huntly 2 | 5 | ✩ | Edinburgh | NJ 558 376 |
| Aberdeen | Ardlair | 31/21+ | | | NJ 5547 2784 |
| Aberdeen | Clatt 1 | 4/5+ | ✩ | Knockespock Ho. (pr.) | NJ 539 260 |
| Aberdeen | Clatt 2 | 5 | ✩ | lost | NJ 5384 2588 |
| Aberdeen | Clatt 3 | 12/31 | ✩ | lost | NJ 5384 2588 |
| Aberdeen | Insch | 5/45+ | § | | NJ 610 302 |
| Aberdeen | Wantonwells | 5 | | Aberdeen | NJ 615 274 |
| Aberdeen | Newbigging Leslie | 17/38* | ✩ | Leith Hall | NJ 604 258 |
| Aberdeen | Percylieu | 41/12 | ✩ | Leith Hall | NJ 535 264 |
| Aberdeen | Rhynie 2 | 5/? | △✩ | | NJ 4980 2715 |

| | County | Name | Symbol | | Present location | Grid reference of original site |
|---|---|---|---|---|---|---|
| 93 | Aberdeen | Rhynie 4 | 31/8+ | ☆ | lost | NJ 4982 2700 |
| 94 | Aberdeen | Rhynie 5 | 39b/5* | ☆ | | NJ 499 265 |
| 95 | Aberdeen | Rhynie 6 | 5/8+ | ☆ | | NJ 499 265 |
| 96 | Aberdeen | Rhynie 1 | 41/31 | § | | NJ 4971 2634 |
| 97 | Aberdeen | Barflat | 31/? | | | NJ 497 262 |
| 98 | Aberdeen | Newton House | 3/45 | § | private | NJ 6623 2972 |
| 99 | Aberdeen | Newton of Lewesk | 6/?/10 | | lost | NJ 7049 2592 |
| 100 | Aberdeen | Logie Elphinstone 1 | 8/3 | | private | NJ 703 258 |
| 101 | Aberdeen | Logie Elphinstone 2 | 8/5 | Ⓗ§ | private | NJ 703 258 |
| 102 | Aberdeen | Logie Elphinstone 3 | 31/8 | | private | NJ 703 258 |
| 103 | Aberdeen | Inverurie 1 | 18/6 /45/5 | §☆ | | NJ 780 206 |
| 104 | Aberdeen | Inverurie 3 | ?/5 | ☆ | | NJ 780 206 |
| 105 | Aberdeen | East Balhalgardy | 5 | | | NJ 7608 2379 |
| 106 | Aberdeen | Drimmies | 12/14* | ☆ | | NJ 742 235 |
| 107 | Aberdeen | Daviot | 8/9* | | Mounie Castle (pr.) | NJ 7595 2800 |
| 108 | Aberdeen | Brandsbutt | 8/45 | Ⓗ | | NJ 7599 2240 |
| 109 | Aberdeen | Keith Hall | 5/41* | | private | NJ 7880 2136 |
| 110 | Aberdeen | Crichie | 31/8 | § | | NJ 779 197 |
| 111 | Aberdeen | Bourtie | 8/5* | ☆ | | NJ 804 249 |
| 112 | Aberdeen | Kintore 1 | 41/4//8/31 | § | | NJ 793 163 |
| 113 | Aberdeen | Kintore 2 | 31/5//31+ | ☆ | Edinburgh | NJ 793 163 |
| 114 | Aberdeen | Kintore 3 | 10/21 | | Edinburgh | NJ 793 163 |
| 115 | Aberdeen | Nether Corskie | 6* | ☆ | | NJ 748 096 |
| 116 | Aberdeen | Kinellar | 1/8 | | | NJ 821 144 |
| 117 | Aberdeen | Dyce | 31/5 | | | NJ 875 154 |
| 118 | Aberdeen | Park House | 23/8* | ☆ | private | NJ 794 984 |
| 119 | Aberdeen | Craigmyle House | ?/44/41 | §☆ | private | NJ 640 024 |
| 120 | Aberdeen | Mar Coldstone | 23/8 | ☆ | private | NJ 4324 0795 |
| 121 | Aberdeen | Tullich | 5/31+ | ☆ | | NO 390 975 |
| 122 | Angus | Baggerton | 45 | ☆ | lost | NO 470 537 |
| 123 | Angus | Inverkeillor | 8/31+ | ☆ | Kinblethmont Ho. (pr.) | NO 638 473 |
| 124 | Angus | Dunnichen | 46/5* | § | Dundee | NO 516 496 |
| 125 | Angus | Aberlemno 4 | 12/31 | | Dundee | NO 524 556 |
| 126 | Angus | Aberlemno 1 | 44/5* | § | | NO 5228 5591 |
| 127 | Angus | Glamis 1 | 37?/44+ | | } both these stones | NO 3937 4654 |
| 128 | Angus | Glamis 2 | 44/41+ | | re-used for Class II | NO 385 468 |
| 129 | Perth | Bruceton | 12/31 | § | | NO 290 504 |
| 130 | Angus | Keillor | 38/5+ | §☆ | | NO 273 398 |
| 131 | Angus | Linlathen | 31 | ☆ | lost | NO 4662 3376 |
| 132 | Angus | Strathmartine | 8/31 | | Dundee | NO 374 361 |
| 133 | Perth | Collace | ?/31* | | Aberdeen | NO 2069 3319 |
| 134 | Perth | Longforgan | 2? | | lost | NO 306 299 |
| 135 | Perth | St Madoes | 13/41//21*//41/44 Ⓗ | | Perth | NO 1964 2120 |
| 136 | Perth | Abernethy | 21/8 | ☆ | | NO 1899 1638 |
| 137 | Fife | Lindores | 4/8+ | | | NO 262 169 |
| 138 | Fife | Strathmiglo | 21/39d | ☆ | | NO 2167 1022 |
| 139 | Fife | Westfield Farm 1 | 6?/22 | ☆ | Falkland Palace | NO 2384 0732 |
| 140 | Fife | Westfield Farm 2 | 6/3 | ☆ | Falkland Palace | NO 2384 0732 |
| 141 | Fife | Walton | 40e/3? | ☆ | Crawford Priory (pr.) | NO 363 096 |
| 142 | Perth | Blackford | 40g/? | | | NN 9243 0980 |
| 143 | Perth | Struan | 5/12? | | | NN 8087 6533 |
| 144 | Midlothian | Edinburgh | 8/5 | ☆ | Edinburgh | NT 250 736 |

# LIST OF CLASS II STONES

## Explanation of notation

/ = pair (as in, say, 17/12). // = symbols on both sides of a stone (as, say, 14/1//18/2).
− = symbols are side by side on a stone (as, say, 6−23).
+ = mirror. * = mirror and comb.
↟ = Figure. ↷ = Animal. ◇ = Horseman. § = Symbol on pillar. H = ogham present

| County | Name | Symbol | Present location | Grid reference of original site |
|---|---|---|---|---|
| Orkney | Brough of Birsay | 6/8/31/40e ↟ | Edinburgh | HY 2398 2850 |
| Caithness | Halkirk | 43−43//15/8 ↷ | Thurso | ND 1309 6205 |
| Caithness | Ulbster | 31/41//8/35d 19/43//3/10 ↷ | Thurso | ND 1255 6879 |
| Caithness | Latheron 2 | 40e/41 ◇H | Edinburgh | ND 1981 3315 |
| Sutherland | Golspie | 17/31//35d/41// 46/8//3/44 H ↟ | Dunrobin | NH 837 002 |
| Ross | Tarbat | 8/21/45/31? ◇ | Edinburgh | NH 915 840 |
| Ross | Hilton of Cadboll | 5/8/2/* ◇ | Edinburgh | NH 8730 7688 |
| Ross | Shandwick | 3/31 ◇ | | NH 8555 7471 |
| Ross | Nigg | 40e/31 ◇ | | NH 8046 7171 |
| Ross | Rosemarkie | 8/8//5/8++ | | NH 737 576 |
| Hebrides | Raasay | 21/8 | | NG 5467 3677 |
| Nairn | Glenferness | 31/8/5/31 ↟ | private | NH 9364 4253 |
| Moray | Brodie | 43−43//31/5 H | | NH 989 584 |
| Moray | Elgin | 5/8 ◇ | | NJ 2159 6285 |
| Banff | Mortlach | 43−43//40e/44 ◇ | | NJ 3241 3924 |
| Aberdeen | Dyce | 8/4−6/5 | | NJ 875 154 |
| Aberdeen | Maiden Stone | 23/31* § | | NJ 703 247 |
| Aberdeen | Monymusk | 19/4 | | NJ 70 15 |
| Aberdeen | Migvie | 5−13 ◇ | | NJ 436 068 |
| Kincardine | Fordoun | /5 ◇ | | NO 7261 7841 |
| Angus | Aberlemno 2 | 23/4 ◇ | | NO 5225 5586 |
| Angus | Aberlemno 3 | 8/5 ◇ | | NO 5223 5555 |
| Angus | Woodwray | 3/18 ◇ | Edinburgh | NO 5185 5663 |
| Angus | Kirriemuir 1 | *18? ↟ | | NO 389 544 |
| Angus | Kirriemuir 2 | 5 ◇ | | NO 389 544 |
| Angus | Kingoldrum | *19/9 ↟ | Edinburgh | NO 334 550 |
| Angus | Cossans | 8/5 ◇ | | NO 400 500 |
| Perth | Alyth | 5 | | NO 2432 4878 |
| Perth | Meigle 1 | 41/45* (39b + 31) ↷◇ | | NO 2872 4459 |
| Perth | Meigle 4 | 31/8 ◇ | | NO 2872 4459 |
| Perth | Meigle 5 | 6/31 ◇ | | NO 2872 4459 |
| Perth | Meigle 6 | 3/9 ◇ | | NO 2872 4459 |
| Perth | Meigle 7 | 5* | | NO 2872 4459 |
| Perth | Rossie Priory | 8/31 ◇ | private | NO 292 308 |
| Angus | Eassie | 31/5 ↟ | | NO 352 474 |
| Angus | Glamis 1 | 4/46 | | NO 3937 4654 |
| Angus | Glamis 2 | 39d/4 | | NO 385 468 |
| Angus | Balluderon | 31/45 ◇ | | NO 374 375 |
| Angus | Strathmartine 3 | 18/31 | lost | NO 378 352 |
| Angus | Strathmartine 5 | 5 | lost | NO 378 352 |
| Angus | Strathmartine 6 | 31 | lost | NO 378 352 |
| Angus | Monifieth 1 | 3/5* | Edinburgh | NO 4953 3235 |

| | County | Name | Symbol | Present location | Grid reference of original site |
|---|---|---|---|---|---|
| 43 | Angus | Monifieth 2 | 39d/8 | Edinburgh | NO 4953 3235 |
| 44 | Angus | St Vigeans 1 | 5/9*    ↑ | | NO 638 429 |
| 45 | Angus | St Vigeans 2 | 3?/?//45/40e | | NO 638 429 |
| 46 | Angus | St Vigeans 3 | 5 | | NO 638 429 |
| 47 | Angus | St Vigeans 4 | 3? | | NO 638 429 |
| 48 | Angus | St Vigeans 5 | ?/5 | | NO 638 429 |
| 49 | Angus | St Vigeans 6 | 5 | | NO 638 429 |
| 50 | Perth | St Madoes | 8–5/31   ✧ | | NO 196 212 |
| 51 | Perth | Logierait | 45   ✧ | | NN 967 520 |
| 52 | Perth | Dunfallandy | 31/?//3/8//8/31 ✧↑ | | NN 9462 5635 |
| 53 | Perth | Fowlis Wester | 5/8   ✧ | | NN 928 240 |
| 54 | Perth | Gask House | 45/46   ✧ | Moncrieff House (pr.) | NO 1328 1932 |
| 55 | Perth | Murthly | 8/31 | Perth | NO 096 392 |
| 56 | Fife | Upper Largo | 5/31   ✧ | | NO 423 035 |
| 57 | Fife | Scoonie | 31/?   ✧H | Edinburgh | NO 384 017 |

Detail of stone from Brough of Birsa Orkney, showing three Pictish warriors.

# LIST OF CLASS III STONES WITH HORSEMEN

## Explanation of notation
✫ = damaged stone.  H = ogham present

| County | Name | Comment | Present location | Grid reference of original site |
|--------|------|---------|------------------|------------------|
| Shetland | Bressay | 1 Horseman  H | Edinburgh | HO 522 424 |
| Ross | Edderton | 3 Horsemen | | NH 719 843 |
| Moray | Burghead 8 | 1 Horseman  ✫ | Edinburgh | NJ 1102 6915 |
| Moray | Drainie 3 | 1 Horseman  ✫ | Elgin | NJ 223 694 |
| Moray | Drainie 13 | 2 Horsemen  ✫ | Elgin | NJ 223 694 |
| Moray | Sueno's Stone | many horsemen | Forres | NJ 046 595 |
| Angus | Menmuir 1 | 2 Horsemen | | NO 534 644 |
| Angus | Menmuir 2 | 1 Horseman  ✫ | | NO 534 644 |
| Angus | Aldbar | 1 Horseman | Brechin Cathedral | NO 574 580 |
| Angus | Inchbrayock 1 | 1 Horseman | Montrose | NO 709 568 |
| Angus | Inchbrayock 2 | 1 Horseman | Montrose | NO 709 568 |
| Angus | Inchbrayock 3 | 2 Horsemen | lost | NO 709 568 |
| Angus | St Vigeans 17 | 1 Horseman  ✫ | | NO 639 429 |
| Angus | St Vigeans 22 | 1 Horseman  ✫ | | NO 639 429 |
| Angus | Monifieth 3 | 1 Horseman | Edinburgh | NO 499 325 |
| Angus | Kirriemuir 3 | 2 Horsemen | | NO 389 545 |
| Angus | Benvie | 2 Horsemen | | NO 333 328 |
| Angus | Invergowrie 2 | 1 Horseman | Edinburgh | NO 348 304 |
| Perth | Meigle 2 | 5 Horsemen | | NO 2872 4459 |
| Perth | Meigle 3 | 1 Horseman | | NO 2872 4459 |
| Perth | Meigle 11 | 3 Horsemen | | NO 2872 4459 |
| Perth | Meigle 16 | 1 Horseman | | NO 2872 4459 |
| Perth | Dunkeld 2 | 2 Horsemen | | NO 025 426 |
| Perth | Dupplin | 1 Horseman | | NO 053 188 |
| Perth | Forteviot 4 | 1 Horseman  ✫ | | NO 052 175 |
| Perth | Dull | 2 Horsemen  ✫ | Edinburgh | NN 806 493 |
| Fife | Mugdrum | 3 Horsemen  ✫ | private | NO 225 180 |
| Fife | Dogton | 1 Horseman | | NO 236 968 |
| Fife | Sauchope | 2 Horsemen | Crail | NO 616 083 |
| Fife | Inverkeithing | 3 Horsemen | lost | NT 130 830 |
| Kinross | Tullibole | 1 Horseman | Edinburgh | NO 055 008 |
| Perth | Dunblane 1 | 1 Horseman | | NN 782 014 |

# The Symbol Stones of Scotland

The ideas in the present book are developed in more detail in *The Symbol Stones of Scotland*, by the same author and also published by The Orkney Press (£5.95 paperback).* *The Symbol Stones of Scotland* analyses the distribution of the symbols and brings out its significance in terms of marriage between lineages. It goes on to work out a possible structure for the Pictish kingship, examines the role played by Christianity, and offers a new explanation for the baffling ogham inscriptions that have so far proved untranslatable. The 254-page book contains 15 pages of photographs and numerous maps and tables. A number of grid references have been updated in the present book, and some minor errors amended. *The Symbol Stones of Scotland* is an ideal way to follow up *The Pictish Trail*.

\* Second Impression 1990 £7.95. Hardback £14.95.